Praise for
The S'mores Cookbook

"An entire book devoted to my favorite treat in the world: s'mores! Even my kids couldn't decide which recipe to make first out of *The S'mores Cookbook*. The images are droolworthy, page after page. Susan Whetzel has written a love letter to every kid at heart!"

—**Catherine McCord,** founder of Weelicious and author of
Weelicious: 140 Fast, Fresh, and Easy Recipes

"Susan's recipes are like a big s'mores-wrapped hug of culinary happiness! She has taken basic comfort to basically wonderful!"

—**Chef Betty Fraser and Chef Denise DeCarlo**,
"the comfort food queens" of Grub Restaurant

"*The S'mores Cookbook* takes me back to a happy place filled with marshmallow clouds and sugary dreams."

—**Chef Ben Ford**, Ford's Filling Station

Published by
Adams Media, a division of F+W Media, Inc.
57 Littlefield Street, Avon, MA 02322. U.S.A.
www.adamsmedia.com

ISBN 10: 1-4405-6527-9
ISBN 13: 978-1-4405-6527-4
eISBN 10: 1-4405-6528-7
eISBN 13: 978-1-4405-6528-1

Printed in the United States of America.

10 9 8 7 6 5 4 3 2 1

Always follow safety and commonsense cooking protocol while using kitchen utensils, operating ovens and stoves, and handling uncooked food. If children are assisting in the preparation of any recipe, they should always be supervised by an adult.

Photography by Bree Hester and Susan Whetzel.

This book is available at quantity discounts for bulk purchases.
For information, please call 1-800-289-0963.

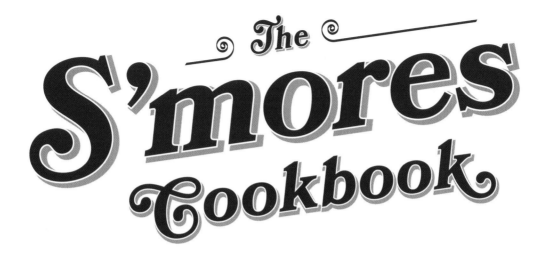

The S'mores Cookbook

From S'MORES STUFFED FRENCH TOAST to a S'MORES CHEESECAKE RECIPE, Treat Yourself to S'more of Everything

SUSAN WHETZEL

Foreword by **CHEF DUFF GOLDMAN, CHARM CITY CAKES**

Aadamsmedia
Avon, Massachusetts

Dedication

For Seven, my lucky charm.

Acknowledgments

A huge thanks goes out to my family—Jon and Seven especially. You always keep me going when I think I can't take another step.

To Bree, who takes the most gorgeous photos—I can't tell you how much I appreciate you and your friendship. You've made this book beautiful.

To my blogger friends—Thank you for the inspiration and for always being there, even when you are terrible influences.

And to Duff—There are no words. Thank you, friend.

Contents

Foreword

The single most defining characteristic of the thought process of American cuisine is that we love to take that which is awesome and combine it with something that is also awesome and be left with a re-imagined something that is more awesome than the sum of its awesome parts. In the more than half-century history of the American classic treat, the s'more, progress has come in fits and starts. A little innovation here, an added layer there, resulting in a few scattered ideas in just how to combine graham crackers, chocolate, and marshmallows in new and exciting ways. But as it occurs with all evolutionary processes, mammoth progress happens in short, violent bursts. This book is a fine example of a culinary evolutionary eruption.

It is only in the last few years that we have taken the s'more indoors. This was a treat that for most of its existence was only available to the initiates of that most American summer pastime, camping. Somehow, it just felt wrong to stack chocolate and marshmallows on a graham cracker and roast it in your fireplace or, heaven forbid, your electric oven. But as tales emerged from young and old alike about the delights of this particular combination of carbohydrates, the lay-abouts and "indoorsy" folk brought down the walls of s'more propriety and, voilà, s'mores became a fixture in our homes.

This transition, from campsite to kitchen, is what I believe paved the woodland path for the culinary innovation that follows in Susan's cookbook. S'mores Coffee Cake, for example, could only happen where there was the what-for for making a coffee cake in the first place, much more readily made in the kitchens of our nation's bakers than in the deep woods where food is carried in (measured in grams) and no unnecessary weight is tolerated. Nobody shook up a S'more-tini after a ten-hour hike. I'm almost positive nobody strapped a bain-marie to her back and made mountain-top S'mores Crème Brûlée.

So, rejoice! Give thanks to our innovators who reclaimed the s'more from the province of open flame and bark-covered cooking utensils. The s'more has been tamed, but not too much. All of Susan's recipes and delicious ideas are crafted to be enjoyed anywhere polite society gathers. But every bite, every whiff, will stir in each and every one of us a not-too-dormant and less-evolved version of ourselves where melty bars of chocolate adhered not only to twice-toasted graham crackers, but the textural symphony of blackened charred ooey-gooey sticky hot goopy marshmallows meant perfection. And don't be shy; after whipping up a batch of S'mores Puff Pastry Mini Tarts, gather everyone around, put the TV on mute, turn the track lights down, and tell a scary story.

—Duff Goldman

Introduction

Just the mention of the word *s'more* conjures up the feeling of cool night air, a star-filled sky, and the feel of a log-filled fire warming our noses. S'mores are, in essence, a memory maker. Chocolate, graham crackers, and marshmallows, transformed magically into happiness; a time machine to our youth and nights spent with family and friends.

Many of us have memories of s'mores from our own childhood—be it camping with our parents or friends by the lake, or with a Girl Scout or Boy Scout troop—there was a night spent by the fire, marshmallows in hand, chocolate smudged on our chins. S'mores evoke such fond memories for so many, and that fondness is what led me to the writing of this unusual cookbook.

Some of my favorite things about living where I do are our spacious backyard, raised garden beds, covered grilling area, and most recently, an in-ground fire pit. My husband is an avid outdoorsman as well as overall handyman, and one weekend he surprised me with an impressive stone fire pit built from native rock and topped with a custom grill grate. Surrounded by large stepping-stones and comfortable chairs, on nice evenings we can build a roaring fire to cook our dinner over, and of course, later on, roast marshmallows. My son has become quite the expert marshmallow roaster, and even has his own special skewer—a gift from a blogging friend. Many nights are spent building gooey, chocolaty s'mores in the moonlight—a memory I hope he will one day look back upon with a smile.

The recipes found throughout this book are all inspired by the original s'more. Marshmallows, graham crackers, and chocolate are featured on every page, and all with different results. You'll find numerous breakfast s'more recipes, a chapter on pies and cakes, another on frozen s'mores inspirations, and even a chapter on s'mores that are perfect for gift giving. I've also included a chapter on gourmet s'mores, in flavor combinations you may have never considered (but should!). One thing you'll find for sure about the recipes in this book, whether it's the S'mores Danish, the S'mores Frappuccino, the crowd-pleasing S'mores Coffee Cake, or the S'mores Stuffed French Toast—they are all delicious, and hopefully each one will take you back to that night by the fire, stick in hand, eagerly awaiting that first bite of heaven. Breakfast, lunch, dinner, parties—every occasion is covered here, so head into the kitchen, experiment, play, and most of all . . . enjoy!

Chapter 1

All about S'mores

Welcome to the wonderful world of s'mores! S'mores are one of the most quintessentially American of all sweet treats, and, you'll be happy to find out, they're one of the most adaptable as well! There are endless varieties of gooey, sweet confections derived from s'mores—everything from refined cakes to quirky drinks! Before you skip to the recipes, take a minute to peruse this chapter and learn about the history and basics of s'mores. You'll learn where the treat came from, how to buy and store all sorts of ingredients, and how to use different appliances to get the results that you want for your s'mores. It'll be one sweet read!

The History of the S'more

Most of us began our love affair with the s'more as children, huddled around a blazing campfire, eager to have our perfectly toasted marshmallow sandwiched between two graham crackers and a mouthful of chocolate. But where did the idea originally come from?

Like many things we know and love as a culture, the s'more has no real known origin. What *is* known is that the s'more was certainly not the first treat made featuring the three simple ingredients of graham cracker, marshmallow, and chocolate. Early in the twentieth century, Mallomars, followed by the MoonPie, both combined the ingredients to create widely popular treats.

With the development of mass-produced marshmallows in the late teens and early 1920s, the s'more became a favorite of campers.

The ingredients were easy to find and easy to transport; the simple dessert offered a wilderness luxury that had previously been unavailable. Despite the campers passing the recipe from one to another for several years, it was the Girl Scouts who are first credited with the official s'mores recipe, which was published in 1927.

Credited to a scout leader, Loretta Scott Crew, who was known for making the treats for the girls, the recipe was printed in the handbook *Tramping and Trailing with the Girl Scouts* (a copy of which reportedly sold on eBay for $250 in 2011). The publication of the recipe was the first time that the s'more had been introduced to mainstream culture, and it quickly became a favorite of adults and children alike. The simplicity of preparation, the ease of obtaining products, and the overall flavor combination seemed to impress everyone, and it soon became a household name.

The actual name *s'more* is thought to be derived as a contraction of the words *some* and *more*—as in, "Give me s'more!"—a chant you are likely to hear when combining the sweet and sticky marshmallow with the crunchy graham cracker and silky smooth chocolate. No one can stop at a single serving! In fact, the s'more is so popular that on August 10 every year, the United States has an official S'mores Day, celebrated by lovers of the campfire treat all around the country.

RECORD-BREAKING DESSERT

The Guinness Book of World Records lists the largest s'more ever made weighed in at 1,600 pounds; it used 20,000 marshmallows and 7,000 chocolate bars. That's a lot of deliciousness!

S'mores Components

The three main components of a s'more—graham crackers, chocolate, and marshmallows—are a delicious combination that work wonderfully together in a variety of recipes and applications. The crunch of the graham cracker, with its mild honey sugariness, paired with the richness of chocolate and sweetness of the toasted marshmallows offer a flavor and texture that blend seamlessly into desserts such as pies, cakes, and ice creams. Breakfast foods are also excellent when inspired by the components of s'mores.

Graham Crackers

The graham cracker was invented in 1829 by Sylvester Graham, a minister in New Jersey. It was originally conceived as a health food, made primarily of unbleached wheat flour, bran, wheat germ, and very little sweetener, if any at all. However, over time, with consumers demanding sweeter products, the commercially made graham cracker has become more like a cookie, flavored typically with honey and various sugars. Cinnamon, spice, and even chocolate are popular graham cracker flavorings.

Many commercially made graham crackers are available in a variety of flavors, and are easily purchased in grocery and chain stores worldwide. You can also make your own. This book contains an easy recipe, which allows a lot of freedom in size, shape, and flavorings. Experiment!

Chocolate Bars

The typical s'more is prepared with milk chocolate, and most consumers tend to associate the snack with the original Hershey's Milk Chocolate Bar.

Chocolate bars as we know them today are a relatively young treat. Although chocolate bars and candy bars had their start in the 1800s, it wasn't until the beginning of the 1900s that the confection became widely available and mass produced. The first wrapped chocolate bar, still relatively unchanged from the original recipe, was Hershey's Milk Chocolate Bar, manufactured by the Hershey Company in 1900. It sold for a mere 10 cents. Other than dropping in price to 5 cents during the Great Depression, the 10-cent charge remained virtually unchanged until the 1960s.

Chocolate, at least the modern-day candy as we know it, is the product of an intense refining process that starts with the fruit of the cacao tree. The beans, which are contained inside the cacao pod, are fermented, dried, roasted, and ground. This process results in two separate products: cocoa butter, which is a smooth, solid fat used in both food and many cosmetics; and chocolate liquor, or the ground, roasted cocoa beans. The type, or "darkness," of the chocolate is determined by the various amounts of cocoa butter and chocolate liquor it contains, as well as the level of sugar and any other ingredients or flavorings added to the mixture.

Chocolate is available for purchase in various forms: milk chocolate (such as the Hershey bar), dark or semisweet, bittersweet, unsweetened, and white. Most consumers find the sweeter chocolates more pleasing to the palate, though many fine desserts are made using the darker varieties. All are made using sugar, cocoa butter, cocoa liquor, milk or milk powder, and often vanilla, with varying levels of sweetness. However, white chocolate contains no actual cocoa solids; therefore, many countries do not consider it a chocolate at all.

VARIETIES OF CHOCOLATE

Unsweetened chocolate: Also known as baking chocolate, unsweetened chocolate is pure chocolate liquor, composed solely of ground cocoa beans. While it smells and looks like chocolate, it has a bitter taste and is not typically meant for consumption on its own. It is best used in cooking, so that it can be mixed properly with sugar to make its taste more pleasing. Unsweetened chocolate is the base ingredient in all varieties of chocolate, excluding white chocolate.

Bittersweet chocolate: The Food and Drug Administration (FDA) defines bittersweet chocolate as chocolate that contains at least 35 percent cocoa solids. Most bittersweet chocolates contain at least 50 percent chocolate liquor, with some containing as much as 75–80 percent.

Bittersweet chocolate has a deep, rich flavor, and lends itself well to a variety of baking needs. Many people often find it difficult to eat on its own, due to the typical lack of sweetness, though it has seen an increase in sales and production over the years. Because the amount of sugar in chocolate is not regulated, one manufacturer's "bittersweet" bar may taste sweeter than another's.

Semisweet chocolate: This is primarily an American term, popularized by Nestlé Toll House's semisweet chocolate chips. Like bittersweet chocolate, semisweet chocolate contains at least 35 percent cocoa solids. However, semisweet chocolate is typically found to be sweeter than its bittersweet counterpart. Again, because there is no regulation of the amount of sugar contained in the chocolate, sweetness will vary from one brand to another.

Milk chocolate: As with other varieties of chocolate, milk chocolate contains cocoa butter and chocolate liquor. The difference is that milk chocolate contains either condensed milk or dry milk solids as well. In the United States, according to the FDA, milk chocolate must contain at least 10 percent chocolate liquor, 3.39 percent butterfat, and 12 percent milk solids. Milk chocolates are typically much sweeter than darker chocolates and typically appear lighter in color with a less pronounced chocolate flavor.

White chocolate: White chocolate gets its name due to the cocoa butter it contains; however, it does not contain chocolate liquor or any other cocoa products. Because of this, it does not have a chocolaty flavor and instead tastes like vanilla or other added flavorings. Federal regulations state that white chocolate must contain a minimum 20 percent cocoa butter, 14 percent milk solids, and a maximum of 55 percent sugar.

CHOCOLATE STORAGE

Chocolate is very sensitive to temperature and humidity, and if possible, should be stored in temperatures that are around 60°F, with a relative humidity of less than 50 percent. Chocolate is known to have "blooming" effects that occur if stored or served improperly. If refrigerated or frozen without proper packaging, such as paper or plastic wrap, chocolate can absorb enough moisture to cause a whitish discoloration, which is the result of fat or sugar crystals rising to its surface. Although visually unappealing, chocolate suffering from bloom is perfectly safe for consumption.

Chocolate should also be stored away from other foods, especially spices or aromatic foods, as it can absorb different aromas. For best results, chocolate should be wrapped and placed in proper storage with the correct humidity and temperature. Most people find that chocolate is best stored in a dark place, such as a cabinet, where light and heat are rare.

COCOA BEANS

The cocoa bean, or cacao bean, is the fruit of the cocoa tree. Cocoa trees grow in hot, rainy climates, and the harvest season lasts several months, or even year round in many locations. Cocoa beans are contained inside the cocoa pod, which, when ripe, weighs in at nearly one pound. It is estimated that one harvester, by hand, can harvest 650 pods in a day. According to the Hershey Company, it takes the equivalent of one pod to make a single Hershey bar.

Marshmallows

Marshmallows are a sweet confection, typically purchased by consumers versus being made from scratch. On average, Americans purchase 90 million pounds of marshmallows annually, and it is believed that more than half of the marshmallows sold during the summer months are toasted. The modern, store-bought variety typically consists of sugar, water, cornstarch, gelatin, dextrose, and vanilla flavoring. Often, manufacturers will add food coloring and flavorings other than vanilla to their original recipes. Pumpkin, strawberry, chocolate, mint, and other holiday-inspired varieties are popular throughout the year in limited editions. Making your own marshmallows, however, opens up a world of flavor possibilities, and is definitely worth the time and effort.

Marshmallows date back centuries, and were even popular in ancient Egypt, where they were considered a delicacy meant only for royalty and the gods. Later, Europeans experimented with them in various confections, despite the difficulty in manipulating the original ingredients, which came from the mallow plant. A milestone in the development of the modern marshmallow was the invention of an extrusion process, created by American Alex Doumak in 1948. This invention allowed marshmallows to be manufactured in a fully automated way, which produced the cylindrical shape that we now associate with marshmallows. The extrusion process involves running the ingredients through tubes and then extruding the finished product as a soft cylinder, which is then cut into smaller sections and rolled into a mixture of finely powdered cornstarch and powdered sugar. Doumak founded the Doumak Company in 1961, and it is still one of the largest manufacturers of marshmallows today.

Most of the current brands of commercially available marshmallows in the United States are manufactured by either Doumak or the Kraft Company, under such names as Jet-Puffed, Campfire, Kidd, and numerous store brands. Sizes range from giant to large, both ideal for campfire roasting, down to small and miniature, most commonly used in hot cocoa and baking applications. Marshmallow creme (particularly the Marshmallow Fluff brand) has also become a popular varietal of the confection.

Toasting and Roasting

While a campfire is ideal for roasting marshmallows for s'mores, it's not always the most convenient of methods. Luckily, there are indoor options that require little effort and produce just as tasty results.

Microwave

The microwave is a helpful tool in our busy lives. Quick meals, defrosting meats, and even baking are all the rage in this modern appliance. But you can also use it for making a great s'more. Just place your graham cracker on a plate, top it with chocolate, a marshmallow, and another graham, and place in the microwave for about

POLAR BEAR TREATS

Did you know that the polar bears at SeaWorld Parks love eating marshmallows? They do! Of course, the bears are fed a healthy, balanced diet at all times by their caretakers, but as a bonus they enjoy marshmallow treats from time to time. Another interesting fact? Though it's hard to imagine a phobia of something as sweet and soft as a marshmallow, there's actually a name for just such a thing. If you're afraid of them, then you are considered to have "althaiophobia."

8–10 seconds. Repeat heating on similar settings until your marshmallow is nice and gooey. Don't expect it to toast, however—the microwave is only good for softening up those marshmallows, not browning them.

Oven Broiler

The oven broiler is probably the most convenient and reliable way to toast your marshmallows indoors. Place your marshmallows or full s'mores on a parchment-lined baking sheet and place under the oven broiler. Carefully stand watch at the oven door—this method takes your marshmallows from golden brown to on fire in a matter of seconds. For softer, less dark results, use a lower rack in the oven, and turn the pan about every 30 seconds to ensure even browning. What's best about the broiler method is being able to make multiple s'mores at once—no waiting your turn!

Kitchen Torch

Available in kitchen supply stores and other home retailers, a kitchen torch, or brûlée torch, is a nice handheld appliance to own. Great for adding the crackle to the top of your crème brûlée, it's also a fantastic way to toast your marshmallows for a s'more. One thing to note— the torch will brown your marshmallow, but don't expect the gooey insides you would achieve from a typical campfire or from the broiler method.

Gas Stovetop, Candle, or Sterno

In a pinch, any of these methods will give you a nicely roasted marshmallow. For the gas stovetop, start with a flame-resistant skewer, and wear a protective glove to avoid getting burned. Keep the heat of the flame on the lowest setting to begin, and increase it as needed to achieve the results you desire.

If using a Sterno or candle, again, take care around the flame. These two methods are a bit more troublesome, especially if the marshmallow drips onto the flame (it happens!). For the curious, the company that manufactures Sterno claims that the gas used for the flame is safe to heat marshmallows over. Use precautions if using other brands or varieties of canned fuel.

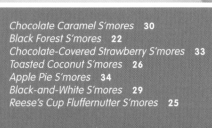

Chapter 2

Not Your Average S'more

There comes a time in everyone's life when the same ol' same ol' just won't do. While the traditional s'more is a tried and true favorite, there are some incredible versions that just beg to be experienced. White chocolate, dark chocolate, peanut butter, fruits, coconut . . . the sky is the limit. Don't be afraid to think outside of the box—sometimes the most unusual of ideas (think Apple Pie S'mores) turns out to be a new favorite. This chapter includes several exciting flavors, from toasted coconut to Black Forest to a Reese's Fluffernutter. These recipes will inspire you to come up with some delicious variations of your own. Experiment!

Black Forest S'mores

Yields: 16 servings

INGREDIENTS

1 can cherry pie filling

32 large marshmallows

32 chocolate graham squares

16 squares dark chocolate

SERVING SUGGESTIONS

You may find the Black Forest S'mores are a bit more difficult to eat, thanks to the pie filling. While completely worth the sticky fingers, you do have options! Consider breaking the graham square into bite-sized pieces and placing it into a serving bowl. Top with the marshmallows and pie filling, then pour a bit of Chocolate Ganache (see Chapter 11) on top. For even more indulgence, a scoop of ice cream would be a welcome addition.

Oozing dark chocolate, chocolate graham cracker, and tart red cherries combine to make an incredibly rich, divinely simple version of the classic Black Forest cake, a decadent chocolate layer cake filled with cream, sour cherries, and Kirsch.

1 Organize ingredients by type: Place the pie filling and marshmallows in bowls and the graham squares and chocolate on platters for ease in assembly.

2 Toast the marshmallows over fire, under the broiler, or using a kitchen torch.

3 Layer 1 graham square, 2 marshmallows, 1 chocolate square, then a heaping spoonful of cherry pie filling over the top. Top with another graham square. Repeat until all the ingredients are used.

Reese's Cup Fluffernutter S'mores

Yields: 8 servings

INGREDIENTS

16 graham squares

12 tablespoons Marshmallow Fluff

8 Reese's Peanut Butter Cups

NOT A FAN OF PEANUT BUTTER?

Whether it's an allergy to peanuts or simply the taste that leaves you unhappy, never fear. Instead of using Reese's Peanut Butter Cups, substitute a mallow-filled chocolate cup. Mallo Cups is a popular brand, and they can be found easily at most chain stores. You can never have too much marshmallow in a s'more!

If you love peanut butter, this is the ultimate treat for you. Forget the fluffernutter sandwich your mom used to make you on Saturday—this s'more is hard to beat!

1 Organize ingredients by type: Place the graham squares on a platter and the fluff and Reese's Peanut Butter Cups in bowls for ease in assembly.

2 Preheat the oven to 400°F. Prepare a large baking sheet with parchment paper. Place 8 of the graham squares on the parchment.

3 Top each square with 1½ tablespoons of Marshmallow Fluff. Press 1 Reese's Peanut Butter Cup into the fluff.

4 Bake until the marshmallow begins to brown and the chocolate starts to melt, about 45 seconds to 2 minutes. Remove from the oven and top each with another graham square.

Toasted Coconut
S'mores

Yields: 8 servings

INGREDIENTS

16 graham squares

8 squares white chocolate

8 large marshmallows

1 cup toasted coconut

HOW TO TOAST COCONUT

The smell wafting from your oven as you toast coconut is heavenly! To toast coconut, simply spread a thin layer of coconut flake onto a baking sheet and place into a 350°F oven. Use a fork to stir the coconut every 5 minutes, until the coconut reaches the desired color. Be careful, as the coconut will quickly go from toasted to burned!

S'mores take a turn to the tropics with the addition of toasted coconut! Paired with the sweetness of white chocolate, this combination will whisk you away to dreams of secluded beaches, sunsets, and sandy campfires. Bon voyage!

1 Organize ingredients by type: Place the graham squares and white chocolate on platters and the marshmallows and coconut in bowls for ease in assembly.

2 Preheat the oven to 400°F. Prepare a large baking sheet with parchment paper. Place all of the graham squares on the parchment.

3 Top 8 of the graham squares with 1 square of white chocolate each. Place a marshmallow on each of the other 8 squares.

4 Bake until the marshmallows begin to brown and the chocolate starts to melt, about 45 seconds to 2 minutes. Remove from the oven, and sprinkle the melted chocolate with toasted coconut. Sandwich each chocolate square with a marshmallow-topped graham square. Serve immediately.

Black-and-White
S'mores

Yields: 8 servings

INGREDIENTS

16 chocolate graham squares

8 squares white chocolate

8 large marshmallows

This s'more is a great example of how simple can also be delicious! Feel free to serve this not only outdoors by the campfire but on a dessert plate with a dainty fork. A bit of whipped cream and chocolate syrup completes the elegant look.

1 Organize ingredients by type: Place the graham squares and chocolate on platters and the marshmallows in a bowl for ease in assembly.

2 Preheat the oven to 400°F. Prepare a baking sheet with parchment paper. Place all of the graham squares on the parchment.

3 Top 8 of the graham squares with 1 square of white chocolate each. Place a marshmallow on each of the other 8 squares.

4 Bake until the marshmallows begin to brown and the chocolate starts to melt, about 45 seconds to 2 minutes. Remove from the oven. Sandwich each chocolate-covered graham with the marshmallow-topped graham square.

SKEWERED

These Black-and-White S'mores look beautiful when prepared in the same style as the S'mores Pops found in Chapter 10. Simply dip your toasted Campfire Giant Roaster marshmallow in white chocolate and roll in the chocolate grahams. For a less formal feel, use large marshmallows versus the giant size. Prepare them the same way by dipping in white chocolate and chocolate graham crumbs, then skewer 3 together.

Chocolate Caramel
S'mores

Yields: 6 servings

INGREDIENTS

6 graham crackers

18 Rolo candies

24 mini marshmallows

The perfect size for snacking! Mini marshmallows, Rolo candies, and a single graham cracker combine to make bite-sized deliciousness!

1 Preheat the oven to 400°F. Organize ingredients by type: Place the graham crackers on a platter and the Rolo candies and marshmallows in bowls for ease in assembly.

2 Prepare a baking sheet with parchment paper. Place the graham crackers onto the parchment. Top the crackers with 3 Rolo candies each, then 4 mini marshmallows.

3 Bake until the marshmallows begin to brown and the candies soften, about 45 seconds to 2 minutes. Remove and serve.

SERVING SUGGESTION

Have a few brownies? You're in luck! Instead of starting your s'more with the graham cracker, begin by placing your brownies onto the parchment paper. Add a heaping spoonful of Marshmallow Fluff, a graham cracker, then the Rolos. Bake at 400°F until the fluff begins to brown. Yum!

Chocolate-Covered Strawberry S'mores

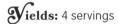 **Yields:** 4 servings

INGREDIENTS

8 dark chocolate cookies

24 strawberry-flavored marshmallows

8 fresh strawberries, sliced

No graham cracker here—it's all about indulgence! Dark chocolate cookies are layered with fresh berries and flavored marshmallows for a tasty and beautifully presented snack.

1 Organize ingredients by type: Place the cookies on a platter, and the marshmallows and strawberries in bowls for ease in assembly.

2 Toast the marshmallows over a fire, under a broiler, or using a kitchen torch.

3 Place 3 marshmallows on top of 1 cookie, then add fresh berry slices on top of the marshmallows. Top with another cookie. Repeat until all the ingredients are used. Serve immediately.

GOING BANANAS

No berries? No problem! Sliced bananas are equally delicious with the strawberry-flavored marshmallows. Simply slice 1 ripe banana and top the toasted marshmallows accordingly. For even more flavor, add a spoonful of Chocolate Ganache (see Chapter 11) to each cookie before topping with the marshmallows.

Apple Pie S'mores

Yields: 8 servings

INGREDIENTS

8 graham squares

12 tablespoons apple butter

½ cup cinnamon baking chips

8 large marshmallows

SERVING SUGGESTIONS

Apple Pie S'mores are excellent served alongside vanilla ice cream. Once baked, place into a serving bowl. Top with a few slices of fresh apple and a drizzle of caramel for a wonderful after-dinner dessert.

Grandma's apple pie has nothing on this incredible s'more! Cinnamon chips atop creamy apple butter pair to give you the down-home flavor of apple pie you crave, in a matter of minutes.

1 Preheat the oven to 400°F. Organize ingredients by type: Place the graham squares on a platter, and the apple butter, cinnamon chips, and marshmallows in bowls for ease in assembly.

2 Prepare a baking sheet with parchment paper. Place graham squares onto the parchment. Top each square with 1½ tablespoons of apple butter, then top with a heaping spoonful of cinnamon chips and 1 marshmallow.

3 Bake until the marshmallows begin to brown and the cinnamon chips soften, about 45 seconds to 2 minutes. Remove from the oven and serve.

Chapter 3

Breakfast S'mores

If there is one favorite meal a day that most people can agree on, it's breakfast. Whether it's a quick muffin before school, a fantastic family-filled Saturday morning feast, or a weeknight "Breakfast for Dinner" treat, breakfast is a wonderfully versatile meal.

The s'mores-inspired breakfast recipes found in this chapter offer choices for every occasion, from a crunchy, graham-encrusted stuffed French toast to deep, dark mini muffins to a gorgeous, hand-braided chocolate and marshmallow-filled Danish. You'll certainly find a recipe (or three!) here that will delight everyone lucky enough to have a seat at your breakfast table.

S'mores Oatmeal

Yields: 4 servings

INGREDIENTS

3½ cups water

1 teaspoon salt

2 cups old-fashioned oats

¾ cup whole milk (warm)

1 tablespoon brown sugar

2 tablespoons unsalted butter

½ cup mini chocolate chips

1 cup mini marshmallows

1 cup roughly crumbled
graham crackers

Nothing warms you up like a hot bowl of oatmeal. Adding all of the traditional s'mores elements makes this an amazing treat the entire family will enjoy.

1 In a medium saucepan, bring the water and salt to a rapid boil.

2 Stir in the oats. Simmer over medium heat, stirring occasionally until oatmeal is nice and thick, about 7–10 minutes. Stir in the warm milk, brown sugar, and butter.

3 Divide the oatmeal into 4 bowls and equally portion the chocolate chips, marshmallows, and graham cracker crumbs into each bowl.

Chocolate
Graham Pancakes

Yields: 6 medium pancakes

INGREDIENTS

¾ cup flour

¾ cup finely crushed graham crackers

¼ cup cocoa powder

1 tablespoon dark brown sugar

1 tablespoon granulated sugar

2 teaspoons baking powder

¼ teaspoon salt

1 egg

1 cup buttermilk

¼ cup melted butter

Simple Marshmallow Syrup
(see Chapter 11), to taste

Expect cheers all around when you serve up stacks of these chocolaty pancakes! The ratio of graham cracker to flour really heightens the s'mores flavor, and of course, the addition of marshmallow syrup brings it all together!

1 In a large bowl, whisk together the flour, graham cracker crumbs, cocoa powder, brown sugar, granulated sugar, baking powder, and salt.

2 In a separate bowl, whisk the egg until very light and doubled in volume. Stir in the buttermilk. Whisk in the melted butter. Pour the wet ingredients over the dry ingredients and stir until smooth.

3 Heat a griddle to medium high. Spray the griddle with nonstick cooking spray. Spoon about ¼–⅓ cup of batter, 3" apart, onto the hot griddle and cook until bubbles start to appear and pop, roughly 2 minutes. Flip and cook until the edges begin to look less wet and shiny. Serve hot with Simple Marshmallow Syrup to taste.

PANCAKE PERFECTION

There is nothing more frustrating than burning your pancakes. To ensure that doesn't happen, try these little tricks: To make sure your griddle is at the right temperature, splash a few drops of water on it. The water should sizzle and burn off quickly. Once that happens, start small. Add a spoonful of batter to the griddle. If it gets too dark on the bottom before bubbles form, it's too hot. Turn back the temperature and wait 5 minutes before trying again.

Graham Waffles

Yields: 6–8 waffles

INGREDIENTS

1½ cups all-purpose flour

½ cup graham flour

4 teaspoons baking powder

2 tablespoons brown sugar

1 teaspoon salt

2 eggs

1½ cups buttermilk, warm

½ cup butter, melted

2 teaspoons vanilla extract

Homemade Chocolate Syrup or Chocolate Ganache (see Chapter 11 for both recipes), to serve

Homemade Marshmallows (see Chapter 11) or store-bought, to serve

These waffles have crispy, graham-flavored goodness! While the recipe is wonderful as-is, consider adding a half cup of chocolate chips to your batter for an extra punch of chocolate. No one will mind!

1 Preheat the waffle iron.

2 In a large bowl, combine the flours, baking powder, brown sugar, and salt. Set aside.

3 In a medium bowl, whisk together the eggs, buttermilk, butter, and vanilla. Pour into the flour mixture and beat until smooth.

4 Pour about ⅓–½ cup batter in the hot waffle iron. Cook the waffles 5–7 minutes, or until the steaming slows down and waffles are crisp and lightly browned on the outside.

5 Serve hot, with Homemade Chocolate Syrup or Chocolate Ganache and marshmallows, as desired.

Chocolate
Graham Dutch Babies

Yields: 4–6 servings

INGREDIENTS

3 tablespoons cold butter

5 whole eggs

½ cup milk

½ cup whipping cream

½ cup all-purpose flour

¼ cup cocoa powder

¼ cup finely crushed graham crackers

⅓ cup granulated sugar

¼ teaspoon salt

2 tablespoons unsalted butter, melted

Large Homemade Marshmallows
(see Chapter 11), to top

Everyone is impressed when presented with this gorgeous, bubbly pancake. Prepared in the oven, it's a joy just to watch the batter bake and rise to unusual heights. Be sure to add the marshmallows quickly to avoid the rapid deflating!

1 Preheat the oven to 425°F. Place the butter in a large cast-iron skillet. Place the skillet in the oven while it's preheating. Do not let the butter burn.

2 Place the eggs, milk, cream, flour, cocoa powder, graham crackers, sugar, and salt in a blender and blend on high for 30 seconds. Turn down to medium speed and slowly add the melted butter.

3 Remove the cast-iron skillet from the oven and pour in the batter. Bake for 25–28 minutes or until the edges rise up and are lightly browned.

4 Cover the center of the pancake with marshmallows and return to the oven to quickly toast. Serve hot, with Homemade Chocolate Syrup (see Chapter 11), if desired.

S'mores Danish

Don't be put off by the amount of ingredients involved or the prep time for this recipe. The majority of your preparation will be allowing the dough to chill between folds. Once you've succeeded making your first from-scratch Danish, you'll know why it's worth the effort!

Yields: 2½ pounds of dough *(enough for 2 large braids)*

INGREDIENTS

For the Butter Block

½ pound (2 sticks) cold unsalted butter

¼ cup all-purpose flour

For the Filling

8 ounces cream cheese, softened

¼ cup sugar

1 large egg

1 teaspoon vanilla

1 cup graham cracker crumbs

2 cups Marshmallow Fluff

1½ cups dark chocolate chips

For the Dough

1 package rapid yeast

¾ cup whole milk, warm

⅓ cup granulated sugar

Zest of 1 orange, finely grated

¾ teaspoon ground cardamom

2 teaspoons vanilla extract

2 large eggs

3¼ cups all-purpose flour

1 teaspoon salt

For the Egg White Wash

1 egg white

1 teaspoon water

Butter Block Preparation

1 Combine the butter and flour in the bowl of a mixer fitted with a paddle attachment and beat on medium speed for 2 minutes. Scrape the sides of the bowl; beat 1 minute more. Cover with plastic wrap. Set aside.

Filling Preparation

2 Beat the cream cheese with the sugar until smooth. Add the egg and vanilla; beat an additional 2 minutes, until well combined. Stir in the graham cracker crumbs, fluff, and chocolate chips. Set aside.

Making the Dough

3 Combine the yeast and milk in the bowl of a mixer fitted with the paddle attachment and mix on low speed. Slowly add the sugar, orange zest, cardamom, vanilla, and eggs. Mix well.

4 Change from the paddle to the dough hook and add the flour and salt, a little at a time, increasing the speed to medium as the flour is incorporated. Knead with the mixer's dough hook for 5–6 minutes, until smooth. If the dough seems sticky, add a bit more flour.

5 Transfer the dough to a lightly floured baking sheet and cover with plastic wrap. Refrigerate for 30 minutes.

6 After the dough has chilled, turn it out onto a lightly floured surface. Roll the dough into a rectangle approximately 18" × 13" and ¼" thick. If the dough is sticky, dust it lightly with flour as needed. Turn the dough to face you lengthwise, and visually divide it in thirds. Spread the butter evenly over the center and right thirds of the dough. Fold the left edge to the right, covering half of the butter. Fold the right third of the rectangle over the center third. This is called a "turn." Mark the dough by poking it with your finger to keep track of your turns. Place the dough on a baking sheet, wrap it in plastic wrap, and refrigerate for 30 minutes.

7 Place the dough lengthwise on the floured work surface. The open ends should be to your right and left. Roll the dough into another approximately 18" × 13", ¼"-thick rectangle. Again, fold the left third of the rectangle over the center third and the right third over the center third. This completes turn two. Refrigerate the dough for 30 minutes. Repeat this process 2 additional times, refrigerating after each turn. Refrigerate at least 4 hours after the fourth and final turn.

Making the Braid

8 Line a baking sheet with a silicone mat or parchment paper. Divide the refrigerated dough into 2 pieces. Work with 1 piece at a time.

9 Place a large piece of parchment onto the work surface and dust with flour. Place 1 dough half onto the parchment and roll into a rectangle roughly 10" × 15". Wrap the other dough half and freeze to use at a later time.

10 Along one long side of the pastry, make parallel, 4"-long cuts with a knife, each about 1" apart. Repeat on the opposite side, making sure to line up the cuts with those on the other side.

11 Spoon the filling down the center of the rectangle. Starting with the top and bottom "flaps," fold the top flap down over the filling to cover. Next, fold the bottom "flap" up to cover filling. Now begin folding the cut-side strips of dough over the filling, alternating first left, then right, until finished. Tuck in the ends.

Proofing and Baking

12 Proof the prepared braid, uncovered, in a warm, draft-free area until doubled in size, roughly 1–2 hours. Near the end of proofing, preheat the oven to 400°F. Combine the egg white and water; whisk to make an egg wash. Brush the braid with the egg white wash and sprinkle with sugar, if desired.

13 Bake for 10 minutes, then rotate the pan and reduce the temperature to 350°F. Continue to bake until golden brown, roughly 15–20 minutes more. Allow to cool on the pan. Serve warm.

S'mores Stuffed French Toast

 **Yields:** 6 slices

INGREDIENTS

6 slices French bread, sliced 1½" thick

1½ cups Marshmallow Fluff

1 cup chocolate chunks or chips

¼ cup milk

1 teaspoon vanilla

2 eggs

1½ cups crushed graham cereal

2 tablespoons butter, for frying

French toast has never been so good!
Chocolate and Fluff are stuffed into thick slices of bread and topped with crunchy graham and even more chocolate. You'll definitely hear cries for s'more!

1 Using a sharp knife, cut a slit in the side of each piece of bread, making a pocket to place the filling. Stir together the fluff and chocolate; spoon the filling into each bread pocket. Repeat until all the bread slices have been filled.

2 In a shallow but wide bowl, add the milk and vanilla, then lightly beat the eggs into the mixture. Prepare a separate bowl with the crushed graham cereal.

3 Heat a large skillet or griddle to 350°F. While the griddle is heating, begin dipping the prepared stuffed bread into the egg mixture, coating thoroughly. Immediately press into the crushed cereal.

4 When the griddle is hot, add the butter to coat the bottom of the pan. Place each slice on the griddle and cook until brown on all sides, approximately 1–2 minutes per side. Serve with Homemade Chocolate Syrup (see Chapter 11), if desired.

S'mores Popovers

Yields: 6 large or 12 mini popovers

INGREDIENTS

3 tablespoons butter

3 eggs

1 cup milk

2 teaspoons vanilla extract

6 tablespoons sugar

⅔ cup all-purpose flour

⅓ cup graham cracker crumbs

Pinch salt

½ cup dark chocolate chips

Mini marshmallows, to top

Homemade Chocolate Syrup (see Chapter 11), to serve as desired

Whipped cream, to serve as desired

Similar in taste to French toast, the popover is a light, puffy delicacy. An eggy batter is transformed into these sky-high treats, popular in many countries. However, making it with s'mores ingredients takes it to an all-new level!

1 Preheat the oven to 375°F. Divide the butter into the cups of the popover pan. Place the pan in the oven for 3–5 minutes while you are making the batter.

2 In a medium bowl, beat the eggs with the milk, vanilla, and sugar, then whisk in the flour, crumbs, and salt. Pour the batter into the butter-filled cups, then evenly add a few chocolate chips to each cup.

3 Place the pan in the oven for 5 minutes, then reduce the temperature to 350°F and continue to bake for another 18 minutes. Carefully open the oven and top with a few marshmallows. Leave in the oven for 4 more minutes. Serve piping hot.

4 To serve, drizzle with chocolate syrup, more marshmallows, and whipped cream, if desired.

WHAT'S A POPOVER PAN?

A popover pan is a pan dedicated to one use: making popovers. It is similar to a standard muffin tin in that it has round cavities. The difference is that a popover pan has deeper cups, which enable a higher loft when baking. If you don't own one, you can use a muffin tin. The popovers will still be wonderful, though they will not puff quite as high.

Mini Dark Chocolate *S'mores* Muffins

Yields: 36 mini muffins

INGREDIENTS

½ cup hot milk

1 teaspoon espresso powder

¼ cup mini chocolate chips

1 egg

1 tablespoon vegetable oil

1 teaspoon vanilla extract

1 cup flour

¼ cup cocoa powder

2 tablespoons graham cracker crumbs

¼ cup white sugar

½ cup light brown sugar

¼ teaspoon baking soda

1 teaspoon baking powder

¼ teaspoon salt

Simple Marshmallow Syrup (see Chapter 11), to top

Need a quick breakfast pick-me-up?
The addition of espresso powder lends a nice kick to these s'mores-inspired muffins. A double batch would be a great idea for breakfast throughout the week!

1 Preheat the oven to 350°F. Line mini muffin tins with mini cupcake papers. Set aside.

2 In large bowl, pour the hot milk over the espresso powder and chocolate chips. Allow to soften for a few seconds, then stir until smooth. Add the egg, oil, and vanilla. Stir until well combined.

3 In a separate bowl, whisk together the flour, cocoa powder, graham crumbs, sugars, baking soda, baking powder, and salt. Pour over the liquids and stir until just combined.

4 Fill the cups about ¾ full. Bake for 8–12 minutes or until the centers spring back when lightly pressed.

5 When cooled, dip in the marshmallow syrup. Garnish as desired.

Chapter 4
Cakes & Pies

Be it a tall, tiered, marshmallow-filled layer cake; an incredibly creamy, chocolate-topped cheesecake; or a dark chocolate decadent pie, you'll find this chapter a source of go-to s'mores desserts. Easy to put together, the recipes in this chapter are ideal for transporting to potlucks, community events, or fun family picnics, and all of them will garner you rave reviews and applause.

Feel free to make these recipes your own by changing up the ingredients to suit your tastes: substitute dark chocolates for milk chocolates; add marshmallows versus fluff; toast, or don't toast; and use cinnamon or chocolate grahams instead of the traditional honey graham. The choices are yours!

S'mores Coffee Cake

Yields: 1 Bundt cake

INGREDIENTS

For the Cake

2½ cups all-purpose flour

½ cup graham cracker crumbs

¾ cup sugar

½ cup light brown sugar

½ cup butter, softened

¾ cup milk

¼ cup heavy whipping cream

2 large eggs

1 tablespoon baking powder

¼ teaspoon salt

For the Filling

¼ cup butter, softened

¾ cup light brown sugar

¼ cup all-purpose flour

1½ cups chocolate chips

1 cup quick oats

Simple Marshmallow Syrup
(see Chapter 11), to top

Thanks to the multiple layers and the dripping marshmallow, this cake is a visual and delectable delight. It's a wonderful and welcome addition to your morning cup of coffee.

1 Preheat the oven to 350°F. Prepare a Bundt pan with nonstick cooking spray. Set aside.

2 To make the cake batter: Combine the flour, graham cracker crumbs, sugars, butter, milk, cream, eggs, baking powder, and salt in the bowl of a stand mixer. Beat on low to medium speed until nicely combined, about 2–3 minutes.

3 To make the filling: In a separate bowl, combine the butter, sugar, and flour until crumbly; stir in the chocolate chips and oats.

4 Pour half of the cake batter into the prepared Bundt pan, rapping on the counter to level. Top with half of the filling. Repeat with the remaining batter, and lastly, the remaining filling.

5 Bake for 50–60 minutes, until set. Pour syrup over the top once the cake is cooled.

$\mathscr{S}$'mores Layer Cake

Yields: 1 (9") layer cake

INGREDIENTS

1 cup hot, strong coffee

6 ounces chocolate chips

¾ cup cocoa powder

1 cup buttermilk

¾ cup vegetable oil

2¼ cups granulated sugar

4 whole eggs

1 egg yolk

1 tablespoon vanilla extract

3 cups all-purpose flour

2 teaspoons baking soda

½ teaspoon baking powder

1 teaspoon salt

6 cups Marshmallow Frosting (see Chapter 11), to ice

2 cups graham cracker crumbs, to layer

Tall, thick, and luxurious, this rustic cake is beautiful and delicious. No need for fancy piping work; let the marshmallow icing swirl and stand center stage.

1 Preheat the oven to 325°F. Grease and flour 3 (9") cake pans. Set aside.

2 In a medium bowl, combine the coffee and chocolate chips. Allow to set for 1–2 minutes to allow the chocolate to soften. Whisk until smooth. Add the cocoa powder and whisk until fully incorporated. Whisk the buttermilk, oil, sugar, whole eggs, yolk, and vanilla extract into the mixture.

3 In a large bowl, whisk together the flour, baking soda, baking powder, and salt. Pour the liquids into the flour mixture and whisk until smooth.

4 Evenly distribute the batter into the 3 prepared cake pans. Bake for 25–30 minutes or until the center springs back when touched lightly. Cool completely on wire racks.

5 Top each layer with 1–2 cups Marshmallow Frosting. Sprinkle 1 cup of graham cracker crumbs between each of the first 2 layers. Top with the remaining Marshmallow Frosting. Toast with a kitchen torch if desired.

Dark Chocolate S'mores Pie

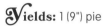

Yields: 1 (9") pie

INGREDIENTS

1 cup sugar

¼ cup cornstarch

¼ teaspoon salt

2½ cups milk

½ cup half-and-half

3 ounces bittersweet chocolate, chopped

4 egg yolks, lightly beaten

3 tablespoons butter

2 teaspoons vanilla extract

1 prepared chocolate pastry shell or pie crust

2 cups marshmallows

Graham cracker crumbs, as desired

This pie features layer upon layer of chocolate, including a chocolate crust; this is for the chocolate lovers in your life! A smooth, dark, creamy filling is topped with toasted marshmallows and a sprinkle of graham to create a deliciously unique s'mores experience.

1 In a large saucepan, combine the sugar, cornstarch, and salt. Slowly whisk in the milk, half-and-half, and chocolate. Cook over medium-high heat until thickened and bubbly, roughly 5–8 minutes, stirring constantly. Reduce the heat to low and cook 2 minutes longer. Remove from heat.

2 Place the yolks in a small bowl; whisk a small amount of the hot filling into the yolks. Pour the mixture into the pan, stirring constantly. Bring to a simmer; cook and whisk 2–3 minutes longer. Remove from the heat.

3 Carefully stir in the butter and vanilla, then spoon the mixture into the pastry shell. Allow to cool to room temperature, then refrigerate for at least 3 hours or overnight. Top with marshmallows. Use a kitchen torch to toast, if desired. Sprinkle graham crumbs over the top for garnish.

Crustless **S'mores** Cheesecake

Yields: 1 (8") cheesecake, or 12 single servings

INGREDIENTS

3 (8-ounce) packages cream cheese, at room temperature

1⅓ cups sugar

3 tablespoons cornstarch

1 tablespoon vanilla extract

¼ teaspoon sea salt

2 large eggs

¼ cup heavy whipping cream

⅓ cup sour cream

½ cup Chocolate Ganache (see Chapter 11)

¼ cup graham cracker crumbs

Marshmallows, as needed

There is no dessert more universally loved than cheesecake, and with very good reason: Cheesecake is incredible. This recipe is especially decadent with the addition of Chocolate Ganache (see Chapter 11) and toasted marshmallows, creating the s'mores flavor we all know and love.

1 Preheat the oven to 325°F and grease or butter an 8" cake pan. Place a round of parchment paper on the bottom. Spray the pan and the parchment with nonstick cooking spray.

2 Place 1 (8-ounce) package of the cream cheese, ½ cup of the sugar, and the cornstarch in the bowl of a stand mixer. Beat on low speed until creamy, about 3 minutes, then beat in the remaining packages of cream cheese.

3 Increase the mixer speed to high and beat in the remaining sugar; then beat in the vanilla and salt. Blend in the eggs one at a time, beating only until completely blended. Be careful not to overmix the batter. Slowly mix in the cream and sour cream until just combined.

4 Pour the batter into the prepared pan. Place the pan in a large shallow dish containing hot water; make sure the water comes about halfway up the sides of the cake pan. Bake the cheesecake until the top is lightly browned and the center is set, about 1 hour. Allow to cool in the oven with the door propped open. Once cooled, remove to the refrigerator to chill completely, at least 4 hours or overnight.

5 Before serving, remove the cheesecake from the pan and place onto a platter or cake plate. Top the cheesecake with the ganache. Sprinkle graham cracker crumbs atop the ganache or around the serving plate.

6 Finally, top the cheesecakes with marshmallows, and toast with a kitchen torch or quickly under the broiler. Serve and enjoy!

INDIVIDUAL CHEESECAKES

This recipe is wonderful when adapted for single servings. If you want individual cheesecakes, use a silicone mold that has 12 cavities and fill each nearly full. Do not use a water bath if making individual cheesecakes, and bake roughly 25 minutes or until lightly browned. Once cooled completely, top with spoonfuls of ganache and a sprinkling of graham cracker crumbs, then garnish with toasted marshmallows.

S'mores Puff Pastry Mini Tarts

Yields: 24 mini tarts

INGREDIENTS

2 puff pastry sheets, thawed

½ cup graham cracker crumbs

1 recipe Chocolate Pudding (see Chapter 11)

2 cups Marshmallow Frosting (see Chapter 11)

The simplicity of this recipe makes it ideal for those lazy Sunday dinners when you just want a quick and stress-free dessert to feed the family. Pop the puff pastry crusts in the oven, stir in some graham cracker crumbs to your prepared chocolate pudding, and top with a dollop of marshmallow frosting. S'mores in delicious pop-able pie bites!

1 Preheat the oven to 425°F. Prepare a mini cupcake tin or mini brioche pan with nonstick cooking spray. Set aside.

2 Roll out 1 sheet of puff pastry; use a round biscuit cutter to cut out 12 circles of dough. Press each into the prepared baking pan. Poke holes into each crust with a fork. Repeat the entire process with the second sheet of dough.

3 Bake crusts for 15–20 minutes, or until golden brown. Remove from the oven and use your fingers or the back of a small spoon to press the puffed crusts back into the pan, creating a cavity for the filling.

4 Stir the graham cracker crumbs into the pudding. Set aside.

5 Once the crusts are cooled, fill each with a large spoonful of pudding, then top with a dollop of frosting. Toast the frosting, if desired.

Chapter 5

Decadent Desserts

When nothing but the best of the best will do, look to this chapter for s'mores-inspired greatness. From chocolaty bread pudding served with sweet marshmallow syrup to buttery, cream-filled éclairs, you'll find decadence in every bite.

Best suited for dinner parties, the recipes found here are a bit more complex and time-intensive, but worth every minute spent on the preparation. Your guests will delight in the familiar childhood s'mores flavors, but relish the adult presentation. S'mores Dip with fresh berries, anyone? Gorgeously layered trifles? Crunchy, sugary, drool-worthy crème brûlée? Go ahead . . . indulge. You're a grownup now.

S'mores **Chocolate** Bread Pudding

Yields: 8 servings

INGREDIENTS

8 slices French bread

1 cup roughly chopped graham crackers

1½ cups milk

½ cup heavy cream

3 ounces semisweet chocolate

1 tablespoon butter

2 large eggs

½ cup granulated sugar

1 teaspoon vanilla extract

Simple Marshmallow Syrup (see Chapter 11), to top

Thick, eggy, sweet, and luscious, bread pudding is an after-dinner delight. Popular especially in the South, bread pudding is surprisingly simple to make and offers a wonderful texture and flavor. The addition of graham crumbs and chocolate to this version results in a s'mores-inspired treat you'll want to make time and again.

1 Preheat the oven to 350°F. Prepare a 9" × 9" baking dish with nonstick cooking spray; set aside. Toast the bread in the oven until just toasted and lightly golden. Remove from the oven. Tear the bread into large pieces and place evenly in the prepared baking dish. Scatter the chopped crackers over the bread pieces.

2 In a medium saucepan, combine the milk, cream, chocolate, and butter. Simmer over medium-low heat, stirring occasionally, until the chocolate has melted, about 4–5 minutes.

3 In a separate bowl, whisk together the eggs, sugar, and vanilla. Slowly whisk in the milk mixture until combined. Pour over the bread and graham crackers.

4 Bake for 25–28 minutes, or until just set. Remove from the oven. Serve warm (or cool) with marshmallow syrup.

S'mores Mousse Cups

Yields: 8 servings

INGREDIENTS

For the Mousse

2 ounces unsweetened chocolate

½ cup sugar

3 tablespoons milk

3 eggs, yolks and whites separated

¾ cup butter

¾ cup confectioners' sugar, divided

Pinch salt

1 teaspoon vanilla extract

To Assemble

1 cup graham cracker crumbs

1 cup tiny marshmallows

Chocolate Ganache (see Chapter 11), to top

1 cup whipped cream

Chocolate shavings, to garnish

These treats offer an elegant presentation and rich flavor without being over the top. An added bonus is the fact that they can be prepared well in advance and refrigerated until just before serving . . . no need to rush around!

1 To make the mousse: In a medium saucepan, melt the unsweetened chocolate over low heat. While it melts, whisk the sugar, milk, and egg yolks in a medium bowl. Once the chocolate is melted, add the sugar/egg mixture. Stir constantly until smooth and thickened, about 7–9 minutes. Remove from heat. Cool completely.

2 In the bowl of a stand mixer, cream the butter on medium speed until fluffy, then add half of the confectioners' sugar and beat for 2 more minutes.

3 Add the cooled chocolate mixture to the butter and beat well; leave in the mixing bowl.

4 In a separate mixing bowl, whip the egg whites and salt to stiff peaks. Gradually add in the remaining confectioners' sugar.

5 Fold the egg white meringue into the chocolate mixture, then add the vanilla. Place the mixture in the refrigerator to cool for 1 hour or more.

6 To assemble: Line 8 dessert glasses up in a row in assembly line fashion. Spoon graham crumbs evenly into the bottom of each glass.

7 Mix the marshmallows into the container of mousse; top the graham crumbs with the mousse. Add a spoonful of ganache to the top of the mousse, then pipe or spoon a dollop of whipped cream to the top of the glass. Garnish with chocolate shavings, if desired.

S'mores Éclairs

Yields: 40–48 small éclairs

INGREDIENTS

1 cup whole milk

1 cup water

1 cup unsalted butter, cut into pieces

1 teaspoon sugar

½ teaspoon salt

2 cups all-purpose flour

7 large eggs, at room temperature

¾ cup graham cracker crumbs

4 cups whipped cream

1 cup Chocolate Ganache (see Chapter 11)

CREAM PUFFS

The same dough used to make éclairs, called *pâte à choux*, is used to make cream puffs. Once you have the dough prepared, simply pipe small rounds onto the prepared baking sheet, or you can opt to use a spring-loaded cookie scoop to make the puffs. Bake cream puffs for 18 minutes, or until puffed and golden. Fill as desired.

Baked but unfilled éclairs and cream puffs can be stored in the freezer for up to 6 months in an airtight container.

1 Preheat the oven to 400°F. Prepare 2 large baking sheets with parchment paper. Set aside.

2 In a heavy-bottomed medium saucepan, bring the milk, water, butter, sugar, and salt to a boil. Once the mixture is at a rolling boil, add all of the flour at once, reduce the heat to medium, and stir the mixture quickly with a wooden spoon. After 1 minute, reduce the heat to low and stir for 3 more minutes. The dough will be smooth and shiny.

3 Transfer the dough into the bowl of a stand mixer fitted with the paddle attachment. Beat the dough for 5 minutes to cool.

4 Add the eggs one at a time, beating for 1 minute after each egg has been added. The dough will separate, but it will come back together after some time.

5 Place the dough into a piping bag with a 1" opening. Pipe the dough into 3"–4" lengths onto the parchment-lined baking sheets. Use a moistened finger to touch up any jagged dough edges, if necessary.

6 Bake the éclairs for 20 minutes, or until puffed and golden brown. Rotate the pans halfway through the baking time.

7 To make the filling, fold the graham cracker crumbs into the whipped cream.

8 Once the éclairs are cooled, fill with whipped cream, using a long, narrow piping tip.

Mini **S'mores** Trifles

Yields: 6 servings

INGREDIENTS

1½ cups crushed chocolate graham crackers

1½ cups Marshmallow Frosting (see Chapter 11), divided

2 cups Chocolate Pudding (see Chapter 11)

1½ cups graham cereal

Homemade Chocolate Syrup (see Chapter 11), to garnish

Trifles are an easy and beautiful way to prepare a variety of desserts. The beauty is in the multiple layers; seen through the glass, no guest will be able to resist it. To prevent the graham cereal from becoming soggy, prepare these trifles just before serving. All of the ingredients can be prepared in advance, then quickly assembled after dinner.

1 Evenly spoon the chocolate graham crumbs into the bottom of 6 small jars or trifle dishes. Layer each jar with 2 tablespoons of the frosting; set aside remaining ¾ cup frosting. Continue the layering with the pudding, followed by the graham cereal.

2 Top each trifle with a piping or spoonful of the remaining ¾ cup Marshmallow Frosting; garnish with chocolate syrup, if desired.

PRESENTATION

Any small glass jar is suitable for this dessert, including a jam or jelly jar. For this presentation, it is easier to place the pudding and the frosting in separate piping bags (without a tip) to aid in cleanly layering the small jars.

✨S'mores Crème Brûlée

Yields: 4 servings

INGREDIENTS

1¾ cups heavy cream

1 teaspoon vanilla extract

4 egg yolks

¼ cup sugar

3 ounces semisweet chocolate, chopped

Sugar, for the brûlée, as needed

Graham cracker crumbs, for garnish

Homemade Marshmallows, Marshmallow Frosting (see Chapter 11 for both recipes), or Marshmallow Fluff, as desired

Crème brûlée is quite simple to prepare, as it is basically a pudding that has been baked. The best part of crème brûlée, though? The crunch of the sugar crust! A quick placement under the oven broiler works best here, but a kitchen torch works as well. Don't forget to add a bit of marshmallow before serving!

1 Preheat the oven to 325°F. Place 4 (4-ounce) ramekins on a baking sheet.

2 Combine the cream and vanilla in a saucepan and place over medium heat. Heat to a simmer; remove from heat.

3 Place the egg yolks in a large bowl with ¼ cup sugar; beat for 2–3 minutes or until well combined. Whisk in the hot cream mixture, about ¼ cup at a time, until you have added half of it to the yolks. Add the remaining cream and whisk until smooth.

4 Stir in the chopped chocolate, and allow to rest for 5 minutes.

5 Whisk the mixture until the chocolate is smooth and thoroughly combined. Pour into the ramekins and bake until the center is set, 12–16 minutes. Remove from the oven, and allow to cool to room temperature before placing in the refrigerator. Chill for 4 hours or overnight.

6 Sprinkle the tops of each ramekin with sugar until evenly coated. Place the ramekins onto a baking sheet, and place under the broiler in the upper third of the oven for 2–4 minutes, or toast with a kitchen torch. Top with a sprinkling of graham cracker crumbs and a toasted marshmallow, a dollop of Marshmallow Fluff, or frosting.

S'mores Dip

Yields: 14–16 servings

INGREDIENTS

1½ cups dark or semisweet chocolate chips

1 (14-ounce) can sweetened condensed milk

⅔ cup Marshmallow Fluff

Homemade Graham Crackers (see Chapter 11), as needed, for serving

Destined to be a party favorite, S'mores Dip is impossibly easy to prepare (three ingredients!), and incredibly versatile. Of course, serve the dip with graham crackers, but also offer your guests a variety of other items to experiment with. Strawberries, bananas, apples, cake, cookies—the possibilities are endless and all are wonderful!

1 Place the chocolate chips in a microwave-safe bowl and heat for 30 seconds. Stir. Pour in the can of condensed milk, and microwave for another 30 seconds. Stir. Repeat in 30-second increments until the chips are melted and the mixture is smooth.

2 Pour the mixture into a serving bowl, then drop spoonfuls of fluff into the bowl. Use a sharp knife to swirl the fluff into the chocolate. Serve with graham crackers to dip.

Chapter 6

Grab-and-Go Treats

For those of us with busy lifestyles, having an arsenal of items we can grab and take on the run is essential, especially when the kids are involved. In this chapter, you'll find some real crowd pleasers, all of which can be made ahead and will be ready to go when you are.

One favorite is the easy-to-prepare S'mores Cereal Bars, which are perfect for an afternoon snack or even a quick breakfast if you are running behind. S'mores-inspired toaster pastries, trail mix, and turnovers are also popular and incredibly easy to make. Simply make a batch of your favorite, wrap in individual serving sizes, and store until needed.

S'mores Granola Trail Mix

Yields: 5 cups

INGREDIENTS

2 cups prepared plain granola

¾ cup dark chocolate chunks

1½ cups graham cereal

¾ cup mini marshmallows

Who says granola has to be so . . .

granola? Kids and adults alike will appreciate this campy treat, whether on the trail, as an afternoon pick-me-up, or while enjoying a late-night movie. Dig in!

Combine all ingredients in a bowl. Store in an airtight container.

TAKE A HIKE

This S'mores Granola Trail Mix is perfect for a day's excursion in the great outdoors. Consider packaging in brown paper bags and tucking away in your backpack for when the hunger pangs strike.

S'mores on a Stick

Yields: 6 skewers

INGREDIENTS

6 Campfire Giant Roasters marshmallows

6 skewers

½ cup chocolate chips, melted

½ cup crushed graham crackers

Unfortunately, there's not always a campfire around when you need one. But that doesn't mean you can't enjoy a great s'more! A baking sheet full of skewered giant marshmallows are only a few seconds away from becoming the s'mores of your dreams—no fire required!

1 Skewer each marshmallow vertically, and place on a baking sheet lined with parchment paper.

2 Place the baking pan under the oven broiler for 25–30 seconds, or until the marshmallows begin to lightly brown. Remove from the oven.

3 Immediately dip the marshmallows into the melted chocolate, followed by a dip into the crumbs. Return to the parchment paper to cool.

STICK IT TO 'EM

Need party favors, and fast? These are great for that! Once your s'mores have cooled and the chocolate has set, place each in a separate cellophane bag. Tie with a cute ribbon, and voilà—instant party favor!

S'mores Cupcakes

Yields: 22–24 cupcakes

INGREDIENTS

1 teaspoon baking soda

1 teaspoon baking powder

¾ teaspoon salt

1½ cups all-purpose flour

¼ cup graham cracker crumbs

½ cup unsweetened cocoa powder

1½ cups sugar

⅓ cup vegetable oil

2 teaspoons vanilla extract

⅔ cup milk

2 eggs

⅔ cup boiling water

1 recipe Marshmallow Frosting
(see Chapter 11)

Chocolate shavings, to garnish

The ultimate in grab-and-go treats!

There's a reason the cupcake is taking the baking world by storm . . . it's the perfect serving size, easy to eat, and requires no fork! For even more graham goodness, consider adding more crumbs to the frosting before sprinkling with shavings.

1 Preheat the oven to 350°F. Prepare 22–24 muffin tins with cupcake liners. Set aside.

2 Stir together the baking soda, baking powder, salt, flour, graham cracker crumbs, cocoa powder, and sugar in large bowl or the bowl of a stand mixer. Add the oil, vanilla, milk, and eggs; beat on medium speed for 2 minutes. Stir in the boiling water to make a thin batter. Pour batter evenly into prepared liners.

3 Bake 18–20 minutes or until an inserted toothpick comes out clean. Cool for 10 minutes in the tins or until completely cool.

4 Pipe or spread the top of each cupcake with Marshmallow Frosting. Garnish with chocolate shavings.

MAKE IT EASY

To quickly fill each cupcake liner, use a large spring-loaded cookie or ice cream scoop. Every cupcake will be uniform, ensuring a batch of evenly baked treats.

S'mores Toaster Pastries

Yields: 6 pastries

INGREDIENTS

2 premade 9" refrigerated pie crusts

1 cup Marshmallow Fluff

½ cup crushed graham crackers

1 cup chocolate chips

If you've never had a Pop-Tart fresh out of the oven, then you are in for a real treat with these s'mores-inspired pastries. Garnish as elaborately as you wish—with ganache, sprinkles, graham crackers—or all of the above!

1 Preheat the oven to 425°F. Prepare a large baking sheet with parchment paper. Set aside.

2 Roll out the refrigerated dough and cut 12 rectangles, roughly 3" × 4". (Reroll scraps as needed.) Place 6 of the rectangles onto the parchment-covered baking sheet. Evenly add a scoop of fluff to each rectangle, avoiding the outer ½" of dough. Top evenly with the crushed graham and chocolate chips.

3 Moisten the edges of each rectangle with water, then top with the remaining 6 rectangles. Press the edges together; crimp with a fork. Prick holes on the top of each pastry to vent.

4 Bake for 14–17 minutes, until golden brown. Garnish as desired.

S'mores Turnovers

Yields: 8 turnovers

INGREDIENTS

1 (17.25-ounce) package frozen puff pastry sheets, thawed

2 cups Marshmallow Fluff

½ cup graham cracker crumbs

2 cups chocolate chips

¼ cup melted butter

Flaky, gooey, chocolaty—turnovers are a cinch to make and are an excellent choice for breakfast on the go. Or, if you are so inclined, serve them warm as a dessert with a scoop of ice cream.

1 Preheat the oven to 400°F. Prepare a large baking sheet with parchment paper. Set aside.

2 Roll out 2 rectangles of thawed puff pastry and trim each into 4 squares. Evenly add a scoop of fluff to one corner of each square, avoiding the outer ½" of pastry. Top each evenly with graham cracker crumbs and chocolate chips.

3 Moisten the edges of each square with water, then fold over the square, making a triangle. Crimp the edges with a fork. Brush melted butter on the tops of each triangle.

4 Bake for 24–27 minutes, until lightly golden brown and puffed. Garnish as desired.

S'mores Cereal Bars

Yields: 24 bars

INGREDIENTS

5 tablespoons butter

6 cups mini marshmallows

8 cups graham cereal

2 cups dark chocolate chunks

You'll appreciate how easy it is to make these incredible cereal bars . . . as you'll be making them often! Loaded with rich dark chocolate chunks, buttery graham cereal, and sweet marshmallow, your crowd will constantly be asking for more!

1 Prepare a 9" × 13" pan with parchment paper, or nonstick cooking spray. Set aside.

2 Melt the butter and marshmallows in a saucepan over low heat, until marshmallows are melted, roughly 3–4 minutes, stirring constantly; remove from heat.

3 Carefully stir in the cereal until evenly mixed, then allow to cool for 1–2 minutes. Stir in half of the chocolate chunks. Press into the prepared pan with a buttered back of a spoon or your fingers; press the remaining chocolate chunks on top. Cool completely. Cut into squares to serve.

Chapter 7

Cookies & Brownies

There is a little bit of kid in all of us, especially when it comes to treats like cookies and brownies. Whether it was an afternoon cookie break courtesy of mom, or a plateful of thick, chewy Sunday brownies courtesy of Grandma, it seems all of us are easily transported to a simpler time once we finally relax and take a bite. The traditional s'mores flavors of chocolate, marshmallow, and graham play perfectly in the baked goods found in this chapter, so no matter which recipe you choose, you'll find yourself reliving those gooey memories in no time. There's something for everyone here!

Oatmeal Chocolate Chip S'mores Cookies

Yields: 3 dozen cookies

INGREDIENTS

1 cup softened salted butter

¾ cup dark brown sugar

¾ cup white sugar

2 eggs

2 teaspoons vanilla extract

1¼ cups all-purpose flour

½ teaspoon baking soda

½ teaspoon salt

¼ cup graham cracker crumbs

2½ cups quick oats

2 cups mini semisweet chocolate chips

12 giant marshmallows, sliced into thirds

The bit of oatmeal used in this batter adds a little more bite and a great texture to the graham-enhanced cookie. Your kids will no longer turn their noses up at an oatmeal cookie!

1 Preheat the oven to 325°F. Prepare a baking sheet with parchment paper; set aside.

2 Using a stand mixer fitted with the beater attachment, cream the butter and sugars at medium-low speed until well combined. Add in the eggs, one at a time, beating well after each addition. Add in the vanilla; combine well.

3 In a separate bowl, combine the flour, baking soda, salt, and graham cracker crumbs.

4 Add the dry ingredients to the wet batter. Mix on low until just combined. Stir in the oats and chocolate chips.

5 Scoop rounded balls of batter onto the prepared sheets. The batter will spread, so be sure to leave ample space between. Bake for 13–15 minutes, or until the edges are very lightly browned.

6 Remove from the oven, and immediately top with a slice of marshmallow. Allow to cool on baking sheets. Before serving, place the pan under the oven broiler or use a kitchen torch to toast the marshmallows.

No-Bake Oatmeal
S'mores Cookies

Yields: 2 dozen cookies

INGREDIENTS

2 cups sugar

½ cup butter

1½ tablespoons unsweetened cocoa powder

½ cup milk

1 cup crushed graham crackers

2 cups quick oats

½ cup peanut butter

1 teaspoon vanilla extract

⅓ cup milk chocolate chips

24 large marshmallows

Ever needed a treat at the last minute? No time? No problem! If you have ten minutes, you have all the time it takes to prepare these deliciously simple cookies. No one has to know they didn't take you all day!

1 In a medium saucepan over high heat, bring the sugar, butter, cocoa, and milk to a rolling boil (or to 205–210°F, using a candy thermometer to measure) for 1 minute.

2 When the mixture is ready, remove from heat and add remaining ingredients (except for the marshmallows), stirring quickly before the cookies set up. Drop by tablespoons, or use a spring-loaded cookie scoop onto parchment or wax paper. Quickly press a marshmallow into the mounded cookie; allow to cool. Toast marshmallows under oven broiler for 25–30 seconds or by using a kitchen torch.

S'mores Stackers

Yields: 3 dozen stackers

INGREDIENTS

36 graham squares (72 crackers)

16 tablespoons butter, melted

⅔ cup sugar

½ cup light brown sugar, packed

2 large eggs

1 teaspoon salt

1 tablespoon vanilla extract

2½ cups all-purpose flour

2 teaspoons baking soda

72 Hershey's Milk Chocolate Bar pips
(6 candy bars)

36 Kraft Jet-Puffed Stacker Mallow
marshmallows

WHAT'S A PIP?

Unwrap your Hershey's Milk Chocolate Bar, and what do you see? All those breakable bite-sized pieces are known as pips . . . and now *you* know!

Love chocolate? A nice big square of chocolate instead of chips in each cookie makes for melting deliciousness in every bite! Play around with this one: Dark chocolate, milk chocolate, or semisweet all work wonderfully in this recipe.

1 Preheat the oven to 325°F. Prepare baking sheet with parchment paper. Place 12 graham cracker squares (24 crackers) evenly on the pan. Allow 1"–2" between squares. Set aside.

2 Using a stand mixer fitted with the beater attachment, cream the butter and sugars on medium-low speed until well combined. Add in the eggs, one at a time, beating well after each addition. Add in the salt and vanilla; combine well.

3 In separate bowl, combine the flour and baking soda.

4 Add the dry ingredients to the wet batter. Mix on low until just combined.

5 Scoop rounded balls of batter onto the graham squares. Batter will spread a bit off the grahams, so be sure to leave ample space between. Bake for 12–14 minutes, or until edges are very lightly browned.

6 Remove from the oven, and immediately top with 2 pips of a Hershey bar and 1 marshmallow. Return to the oven for 2–3 minutes. Remove from the oven and allow to cool on cooling racks. Repeat with remaining graham squares. Before serving, place the pan under the oven broiler or use a kitchen torch to toast the marshmallows.

Gluten-Free **S'mores** Chocolate Chunksters

Yields: 18 large cookies

INGREDIENTS

8 tablespoons butter, softened

⅔ cup dark brown sugar

½ cup white sugar

1 egg

2 teaspoons vanilla extract

1¾ cups all-purpose gluten-free flour

¼ teaspoon baking soda

¼ teaspoon salt

¼ cup gluten-free graham crackers, broken

1½ cups semisweet chocolate chunks

2 cups mini marshmallows

If you or a loved one cannot tolerate gluten, this recipe is an excellent s'mores alternative. No matter what the reason, the elimination of gluten from your diet doesn't have to mean giving up incredible cookies, like these Gluten-Free S'mores Chocolate Chunksters.

1 Preheat the oven to 325°F. Prepare a baking sheet with parchment paper; set aside.

2 Using a stand mixer fitted with the beater attachment, cream the butter and sugars on medium-low speed until well combined. Add in the eggs, one at a time, beating well after each addition. Add in the vanilla; combine well.

3 In separate bowl, combine the flour, baking soda, and salt.

4 Add the dry ingredients to the wet batter. Mix on low until just combined. Stir in the broken graham crackers and chocolate chunks.

5 Scoop rounded balls of batter onto prepared sheets. Batter will spread, so be sure to leave ample space between. Bake for 13–15 minutes, or until edges are very lightly browned.

6 Remove from the oven, and immediately add a few marshmallows to each cookie, pressing down. Return to the oven for 2–3 minutes. Remove from the oven and allow to cool on baking sheets.

Crock-Pot *S'mores* Brownies

Yields: 16 brownies

INGREDIENTS

⅓ cup semisweet chocolate chips

10 tablespoons butter

2 large eggs

1 teaspoon vanilla extract

1¼ cups sugar

3 tablespoons unsweetened cocoa powder

¼ teaspoon salt

¾ cup all-purpose flour

16–18 individual graham crackers

2 cups milk chocolate chips

2 cups Marshmallow Fluff (more as desired)

Set it and forget it! No need to watch over your oven or worry about heating up your kitchen in the summer—you can make brownies using your slow cooker! This recipe is especially perfect for those "edge lovers" out there, as the method ensures a nice outer crust.

1 Line a Crock-Pot with aluminum foil for easy removal of brownies once cooked.

2 In a small saucepan over medium heat, or in a microwave, melt the chocolate and butter until smooth. Allow to cool slightly.

3 In a separate bowl, beat the eggs, vanilla, and sugar. Slowly add in the chocolate mixture until well combined. In a small bowl, sift together the cocoa, salt, and flour. Add the mixture to the rest of the batter. Do not overmix.

4 Pour roughly half of the batter into the prepared Crock-Pot. Top with whole graham crackers, breaking and piecing together at the edges as needed to fully cover the brownie batter. Sprinkle chocolate chips on top of the graham crackers, then top with the remaining brownie batter.

5 Put a lid on the Crock-Pot and cook on low for 1½ hours. Check brownies after 1½ hours. The tops will look undercooked, but a tug on the foil will help determine doneness. If the brownies lift easily without buckling, remove from the Crock-Pot and allow to cool. If they buckle, allow to bake for 15 more minutes, checking again until ready to remove.

6 Once cooled, top with Marshmallow Fluff and place under an oven broiler for 30–60 seconds, until the marshmallows are toasted. Watch closely as marshmallow can quickly burn. Remove from the oven, cut, serve, and enjoy.

Cream Cheese Swirl *S'mores* Brownies

Yields: 16 brownies

INGREDIENTS

For the Brownie Layer

3 ounces dark or semisweet chocolate, chopped

10 tablespoons butter

2 large eggs

2 teaspoons vanilla extract

1¼ cups sugar

2 tablespoons unsweetened cocoa powder

¼ teaspoon salt

½ cup all-purpose flour

3 cups mini marshmallows

For the Cheesecake Layer

8 ounces cream cheese, softened

⅓ cup sugar

Pinch salt

1 large egg

2 teaspoons vanilla extract

Chewy, fudgy, and not at all cakelike, these brownies will have you drooling for more. The creamy cheesecake layer coupled with a thick pile of marshmallows on top are the ideal way to bring the taste of the campfire indoors. Dig in!

1 Preheat the oven to 350°F. Prepare an 8" × 8" baking pan with parchment paper long enough to hang over on two sides, making it easier to remove from the pan once baked. Spray the pan and paper with nonstick cooking spray.

2 In small saucepan over medium heat, or in the microwave, melt the chocolate and butter until smooth. Allow to cool slightly. In a separate bowl, beat the eggs, vanilla, and the sugar. Slowly add in the chocolate mixture until well combined. In a small bowl, sift together the cocoa, salt, and flour. Add the mixture to the rest of the batter. Do not overmix. Pour the batter into the prepared baking pan.

3 For the cheesecake layer, beat the ingredients together until smooth. Pour over the brownie batter. Use a sharp knife to swirl together.

4 Bake 60–70 minutes, or until just set and a toothpick inserted comes out clean. Top with marshmallows. Before serving, place the pan under an oven broiler or use a kitchen torch to toast the marshmallows.

Gluten-Free Layered
S'mores Brownies

Yields: 8 thick brownie slices

INGREDIENTS

2 ounces semisweet chocolate chips

8 tablespoons butter, divided

1 extra-large egg

2 teaspoons vanilla extract

⅔ cup sugar

2 tablespoons unsweetened cocoa powder

¼ teaspoon salt

½ cup gluten-free all-purpose flour

⅓ cup gluten-free graham cracker crumbs

3 full-size Hershey's Special Dark Mildly Sweet Chocolate Bars

3 cups large marshmallows, halved (or homemade)

This recipe features a thick brownie bottom, topped with buttery graham crumbs (gluten-free, of course!), full-sized Hershey bars, more brownie, then mountains of toasted marshmallow. Does life get any better?

1 Preheat the oven to 350°F. Prepare a standard loaf pan with parchment paper long enough to hang over on two sides. Spray the pan and paper with nonstick cooking spray.

2 In a small saucepan over medium heat, or in the microwave, melt the chocolate and 6 tablespoons of butter until smooth. Allow to cool slightly. In a separate bowl, beat the egg, vanilla, and sugar. Slowly add in the chocolate mixture until well combined.

3 In a small bowl, sift together the cocoa, salt, and flour. Add the mixture to rest of the batter. Do not overmix. Pour roughly half of the batter into the prepared baking pan.

4 In a small bowl, melt the remaining 2 tablespoons butter, then combine with the graham crumbs. Sprinkle the mixture over the brownie layer in the baking pan. Top with Hershey bars until the batter is completely covered. Pour the remaining brownie batter on top.

5 Bake 45 minutes, or until just set and no longer shaky in the center of the pan. Top with marshmallows. Before serving, place the pan under an oven broiler or use a kitchen torch to toast the marshmallows. Cut into large slices.

S'mores Macarons

Yields: 2 dozen macarons

INGREDIENTS

1 cup powdered sugar

2 ounces almonds, pulverized

1 teaspoon graham cracker crumbs

3 tablespoons unsweetened Dutch-process cocoa powder

2 large egg whites, at room temperature

5 tablespoons granulated sugar

Marshmallow Frosting (see Chapter 11), to fill

Graham cracker crumbs, to fill

FILLING A PIPING BAG

With a delicate meringue, it's sometimes difficult to carefully fill a piping bag, especially if you are alone. It helps to find a tall glass to place the empty bag in, fold the edges over, and proceed to fill from there. Do not overfill the pastry bag; it is better in the case of macarons to refill as needed.

A gift from our friends in France, macarons are light, airy cookies, as delicate as a cookie can be, but full of intense flavor. Filled with marshmallow icing and a bit of graham, you'll indulge in the classiest of s'mores. *Bon appétit!*

1 Preheat the oven to 375°F. Line 2 baking sheets with parchment paper and prepare a pastry bag with a plain tip (about ½").

2 Place the powdered sugar, pulverized almonds, 1 teaspoon crumbs, and cocoa in a food processor. Pulse for 2 minutes, or until uniform. Stir the bottom of the bowl to fully incorporate all of the mixture. Pulse again as necessary.

3 In the bowl of a stand mixer, make a meringue by beating the egg whites until soft peaks form. While whipping, add in the granulated sugar until stiff peaks form, about 2 minutes. You should be able to turn the bowl upside down without the meringue moving.

4 Carefully fold the dry ingredients, in two batches, into the meringue with a rubber spatula. When the mixture is just barely uniform, scoop the batter into the pastry bag.

5 Pipe the batter on the parchment-lined baking sheets in 1" circles, leaving roughly 1" in between. Rap the baking sheet firmly on the countertop to flatten the macarons, then allow to rest for 20 minutes.

6 Bake for 15–18 minutes; remove from the oven and allow to cool on a baking sheet. Once cooled, fill by piping or spreading each macaron with a bit of frosting and a sprinkle of graham cracker crumbs.

Chapter 8

Chilly

S'mores

Who says your s'mores have to be hot? The flavors created by combining the traditional s'mores ingredients lend itself well to the world of frozen treats. Frozen yogurt, marshmallow ice cream (yes!), or even an ice cream pie will soon be on your list of favorite s'mores treats.

Several of these recipes require an ice cream maker. There are many brands available, both online and in big-box or housewares stores. Most will prepare one quart at a time and are simple to use—just freeze the container, plug in the machine, and fill the bowl with your prepared ingredients. KitchenAid makes an attachment for use with their stand mixers, should you have one and choose not to purchase an additional countertop appliance.

Toasted Marshmallow *S'mores* Ice Cream

Yields: 1 quart

INGREDIENTS

1 (10-ounce) bag marshmallows

1 cup half-and-half

½ cup whole milk

2½ cups heavy cream

¼ cup powdered sugar

1 tablespoon vanilla extract

1 cup mini chocolate chips

1 cup crushed graham crackers

This is the simplest of ice creams to make—just combine and churn for an unusual and delicious frozen treat!

1 Place the marshmallows onto a baking sheet lined with parchment. Place under the oven broiler until just toasted, about 45 seconds. Remove from the oven.

2 In a large pot, combine the half-and-half and milk with the toasted marshmallows. Cook over medium heat, stirring constantly until the marshmallows have melted. Remove from heat and let cool for 5 minutes. Chill thoroughly in the refrigerator, at least 1 hour. The mixture will thicken a bit.

3 While the mixture is chilling, whip the heavy cream to soft peaks. Whip in the sugar and vanilla until incorporated. Do not overwhip.

4 Once the marshmallow mixture is cooled, fold into the whipped cream. Place in an ice cream maker and follow the manufacturer's instructions for freezing. Toward the end of churning, slowly add in the chocolate chips and graham cracker crumbs. Freeze before serving.

Double Chocolate
mores Ice Cream Pie

Yields: 1 (9") pie

INGREDIENTS

¾ cup Chocolate Ganache (see Chapter 11)

1 baked graham tart shell or pie crust

4 cups milk chocolate ice cream, slightly softened

3 cups Marshmallow Meringue (see Chapter 11)

In this recipe, layers upon layers of chocolate meld to provide one heck of a rich delight. You could never go wrong with a bit of chocolate syrup on the side.

1 Spread a layer of Chocolate Ganache over the pie shell. Layer the chocolate ice cream into the prepared pie shell.

2 Allow to freeze for 30 minutes.

3 Add the meringue, piling high in the center.

4 Freeze until set. Remove from the freezer 10 minutes before serving. Toast the meringue using a kitchen torch quickly just before serving, if desired.

S'mores Buddy

Yields: 4 cones

INGREDIENTS

4 sugar cones

1 cup Marshmallow Fluff

3 cups vanilla ice cream

1 cup chocolate Magic Shell

¼ cup crushed graham crackers

¼ cup miniature marshmallows, if desired

Who can resist an ice cream cone? Filled with Marshmallow Fluff, vanilla ice cream, then topped with a chocolate shell, mini marshmallows, and a little graham, and you've got a chilly campfire favorite.

1 Evenly fill each cone with fluff, then a scoop of ice cream.

2 Dip the scoop in chocolate, then roll in graham and marshmallows, if desired.

S'mores
Chocolate Sherbet

 ields: 1 quart

INGREDIENTS

1¼ cups sugar

1 cup water

½ cup heavy cream

¾ cup Dutch-process cocoa powder

1 tablespoon vanilla extract

2 cups marshmallows

1 cup crushed graham crackers

Chocolate sherbet is a wonderful way to get a chocolate fix without the effort of making full-on ice cream. Just quickly combine and enjoy!

1 Combine all the ingredients, except the marshmallows and graham crackers, in a food processor or blender and purée until very smooth.

2 Refrigerate until thoroughly chilled.

3 Add the mixture to an ice cream maker and follow the manufacturer's instructions for freezing. Toward the end of churning, stir in the marshmallows and the crushed graham crackers. Freeze thoroughly.

WHAT *IS* SHERBET?

Many people, including chefs, tend to use sorbet and sherbet interchangeably. Both sorbets and sherbets contain very few ingredients and are primarily composed of fruit and sugar or syrup. According to the FDA, sherbets have a milk fat content of between 1–2 percent, while sorbets, technically labeled "water ices," can be prepared with the same ingredients as sherbets except they can't have milk or milk-derived ingredients and no egg ingredients other than egg whites. You will find that removing the sorbet or sherbet from the freezer 8–10 minutes before serving aids in scooping, as both freeze harder than ice creams or gelato.

Chocolate S'mores Frozen Yogurt

Yields: 1 quart

INGREDIENTS

3 cups Greek yogurt

1 cup plain whole yogurt

8 ounces milk chocolate chips, melted

8 ounces semisweet chocolate chips, melted

¼ cup light corn syrup

1 teaspoon vanilla extract

¼ cup melted butter

1 cup graham cracker crumbs

1 cup Marshmallow Fluff

The combination of different chocolates makes for a nice flavor, but feel free to choose all dark or all milk, or any variation, to suit your own taste.

1 Place yogurts, chocolate chips, corn syrup, and vanilla in a blender or food processor and blend until smooth.

2 Use a fork to combine the butter and graham cracker crumbs; set aside.

3 Add the chocolate mixture to an ice cream maker and follow the manufacturer's instructions for freezing. Toward the end of churning, stir in the buttered graham cracker crumbs and Marshmallow Fluff. Freeze thoroughly.

Chapter 9
Drinks

Of course, hot chocolate comes to mind immediately when thinking of chocolaty drinks, the basis for any s'mores-inspired recipe. But don't stop there! Coffee lovers will adore the grown-up S'mores Frappuccino, a recipe that will give their favorite coffeehouse a run for its money. Thick, icy, and full of s'mores goodness, this coffee-kicked beverage will change many morning routines! On a similar note, the childhood-craving grownups in all of us will flock to the S'more-tini, destined to be a new favorite party cocktail. Campfire-delicious without the fire!

The kids haven't been forgotten, though! Look to the fun Kid-Friendly S'mores Chocolate Milk, as well as the ever-popular S'mores Milkshake to keep the kiddos singing your praises.

S'more-tini

Yields: 2 martinis

INGREDIENTS

¼ cup chocolate chips, melted

¼ cup graham cracker crumbs, for dipping

3 ounces marshmallow-flavored vodka

3 ounces chocolate liqueur

2 tablespoons chocolate syrup

6 ounces whipping cream

Ice, as needed

2 skewers toasted marshmallows (optional)

Sip your cares away by the campfire (or not!) with this decadent s'mores-inspired martini. Perfect for a girls night in, movie night, or just plain Wednesday. Enjoy!

1 Place the melted chocolate and graham cracker crumbs on 2 separate flat dishes. Dip the rims of the glasses into the melted chocolate, then immediately into the crumbs. Set aside to dry.

2 Combine the vodka, chocolate liqueur, syrup, and cream in a large glass or cocktail shaker. Add ice, cover with another glass, then shake vigorously to chill. Strain into prepared glasses.

3 Garnish with marshmallow skewers, if desired.

PARTY TIME, PLAN AHEAD

Having a large group over? Prepare the rims of the glasses in advance and keep them set aside to save time later. You can also multiply the recipe in a pitcher, and keep it stored in the refrigerator until party time. When the guests arrive, add the ice, shake, and pour through a strainer into the glasses. Add your garnish, and have fun!

S'mores Milkshake

Yields: 2 milkshakes

INGREDIENTS

4 cups vanilla ice cream

2 cups chocolate milk

½ cup Marshmallow Fluff

3 tablespoons graham cracker crumbs

Marshmallows, to top

Chocolate squares, to top

Like your drinks cold? The S'mores Milkshake is the perfect solution. A quick whirl of the blender, a few toasted marshmallows on top, and voilà—you're a straw's length from chocolaty heaven.

1 Place the ice cream, milk, fluff, and crumbs into a blender and pulse until well combined and smooth.

2 Pour into 2 glasses; top with marshmallows. Toast using a kitchen torch, if desired. Add a square of chocolate before serving.

Kid-Friendly *S'mores* Chocolate Milk

Yields: 1 (8-ounce) glass

INGREDIENTS

Melted chocolate and graham crumbs for rim, if desired

8 ounces 2 percent or whole milk

2 tablespoons Homemade Chocolate Syrup (see Chapter 11)

1 teaspoon graham cracker crumbs

Miniature marshmallows, to top

The young ones love all things s'mores, and this drink is no exception. If your child balks at the idea of drinking a glass of milk, this may be the way to encourage him or her to try it.

1 If desired, garnish the rim of glass with melted chocolate and graham crumbs, then place the milk, syrup, and crumbs into the glass. Stir until combined.

2 Top with marshmallows and serve.

S'mores Frappuccino

Yields: 1 (12-ounce) glass

INGREDIENTS

¼ cup hot espresso

4 teaspoons sugar

1 tablespoon cocoa powder

¼ cup Marshmallow Fluff

⅓ cup milk

2 cups crushed ice

Whipped cream, to top

Graham cracker crumbs, to top

Homemade Chocolate Syrup (see Chapter 11), to top

Avoid the line at the crowded coffee house—this recipe will cost less than half of what you'll pay for your go-to fancy Frappuccino. (And it tastes better as well!)

1 Combine the espresso, sugar, and cocoa in a blender and pulse for 10 seconds. Add Marshmallow Fluff and pulse an additional 20 seconds. Add the milk and ice and blend well.

2 Pour into a glass, then top with whipped cream, graham cracker crumbs, and syrup, if desired.

S'mores Hot Chocolate

Yields: 1 (10-ounce) serving

INGREDIENTS

8 ounces whole milk

¼ cup semisweet chocolate chips, melted

1½ teaspoons sugar

Marshmallows or Marshmallow Fluff, to top

Graham cracker crumbs, as desired

There is nothing more rewarding and soothing on a cold winter's day than a steaming cup of hot chocolate. Made with only a handful of ingredients, this s'mores version is no exception. Curl up by the fire, grab a loved one, and enjoy.

1 Heat the milk in a small saucepan over medium heat until just simmering. Remove from heat.

2 Stir in the chocolate chips and sugar until well combined and smooth. Top with the marshmallows or fluff. Garnish with graham crumbs, if desired.

FROTHY

This easy recipe is taken up a notch if you own a frother or latte maker. Simply follow your manufacturer's instructions in your latte machine, or use a handheld frother to combine the milk with the sugar and chocolate. You'll have incredibly smooth and silky (and frothy!) hot chocolate that no one will be able to resist!

Chapter 10

Giftable S'mores

There are dozens of holidays throughout the year that require a small gift of some sort, be it Valentine's Day, Teacher Appreciation Day, or even Halloween. Other occasions crop up unexpectedly, and a quick present is often needed.

The projects and recipes in this chapter are ideal for such events, as all are quick and inexpensive, yet all are thoughtful and always well received. Who wouldn't love a s'mores gift? From the simple S'mores Pops, wrapped prettily as a Valentine, to a box full of s'mores ingredients just perfect for a small get-together, you'll find an answer for that occasion without breaking the bank (or your back) to put together. Be playful with your decorations—a little ribbon goes a long way!

S'mores Pops

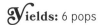**ields:** 6 pops

INGREDIENTS

12 large graham cracker rectangles (48 total crackers)

36 Hershey's Milk Chocolate Bar pips (3 bars)

6 sucker or popsicle sticks

6 Campfire Giant Roasters marshmallows, sliced into thirds

6 cellophane bags

Ribbon, to tie bags, as needed

This is the perfect way to show you care . . . s'mores on a stick! Simple to put together, and great-looking wrapped in a clear cellophane bag, your recipient will love this thoughtful and decadent gift!

1 Preheat the oven to 375°F. Prepare a baking sheet with parchment paper.

2 Place 1 rectangle (4 attached crackers) face down on the parchment. Repeat with 5 more rectangles. Top each rectangle with 6 pips of chocolate, followed by a sucker stick, then 3 slices of marshmallow.

3 Bake for 2–4 minutes, or until the marshmallow starts to puff and the chocolate softens. Remove from the oven and immediately top each with another graham cracker rectangle. Allow to cool.

4 If desired, use a kitchen torch to toast the marshmallow edges. Place a S'mores Pop in a cellophane bag; tie with ribbon.

BE MINE

Consider tying these cute pops up with pink and red ribbon for the sweetheart in your life! A classroom full of kids (or an office full of adults) would love to be your Valentine if presented with a treat like this. Add a fun label or prepurchased sticker to mark the special holiday. Get creative!

S'mores Party Kit

Yields: 1 gift set

INGREDIENTS

12 Hershey's Kisses Milk Chocolates

12 graham cracker squares (your favorite variety)

12 Jet-Puffed StackerMallow marshmallows

1 decorative box with lid

Ribbon, to tie box, as needed

What a great "Welcome Summer" gift! Pack up a few of these easy boxes and hand them out to your child's teacher, coach, or camp counselor to wish them all the best for Open S'mores Season!

1 Place the individual ingredients into the box, leveling as you go.

2 Top securely with a lid; attach the ribbon and label as desired.

S'mores Bars in Jars

Yields: 1 gift jar

INGREDIENTS

1 large Weck or Mason jar

Ingredients for 1 batch S'mores Cereal Bars, without butter (see Chapter 6)

Ribbon, to tie instruction label

What could be easier than preparing the ingredients for S'mores Cereal Bars and layering them into a gorgeous jar? It's a gift your recipient will love receiving, love making, and, of course, love eating! Be sure to add a special recipe tag to the jar so that the recipient knows just what to do . . . it adds a lot of charm as well as information!

1 Place all the items in a jar, separating into sections to suit the jar size.

2 Place a lid on the jar; tie with decorative ribbon. Decorate with labels, if desired.

ℬ'mores Popcorn Bags

Yields: 10 gift bags

INGREDIENTS

1 cup semisweet chocolate chips, melted

½ cup crushed graham cracker crumbs

8 cups caramel popcorn

½ cup white chocolate chips, melted

2 cups mini marshmallows

10 cellophane gift bags

Ribbon, to tie bags, as needed

Feel free to make your own caramel popcorn for this amazing treat, but store-bought works amazingly well and tends to hold up and look nicer in the gift bags. Either way, it's a win-win situation!

1 Cover the counter with parchment paper. Drizzle the parchment with melted semisweet chocolate, and immediately sprinkle with graham cracker crumbs and popcorn, making as even a layer as possible.

2 Drizzle the white chocolate over the popcorn; allow to dry. Once dry, pour the popcorn from the parchment into a large bowl; add marshmallows.

3 Divide evenly into cellophane bags, and tie with decorative ribbon.

Chapter 11

Essential S'mores Recipes

Without the recipes in this chapter, there would be *no s'mores*! While you can certainly buy most items in the grocery store, there comes a great sense of pride and accomplishment in being able to make many of these items from scratch. Marshmallows, for example, are easily purchased, but there is just no comparison in flavor to a homemade recipe.

Marshmallow Frosting, Chocolate Pudding, and Chocolate Ganache are other essential recipes you'll need to keep close at hand for creating many of the treats throughout this book. Master them!

Marshmallow
Meringue

Yields: 2 cups

INGREDIENTS

¾ cup sugar

1½ tablespoons corn syrup

2 ounces water

6 egg whites

Fluffy, airy, and not terribly sweet, Marshmallow Meringue is much more mellow than its icing counterpart. It serves as a wonderful addition to pies, where you may prefer a little less sweetness.

1 In a heavy-bottomed saucepan, combine the sugar, corn syrup, and water and heat to 240°F (soft ball stage). When the mixture approaches 220°F, start to whip the egg whites on medium-high speed until soft peaks form. By the time you achieve soft peaks, the sugar should be at 240°F.

2 Turn the mixer speed down to medium low, and add the hot sugar into the egg whites in a slow, steady stream. Once all of the sugar is incorporated, turn the mixer back to medium high and beat for 15 minutes to cool. Chill the meringue and add to a piping bag for use once cool.

Chocolate Ganache

Yields: scant 1 cup

INGREDIENTS

½ **cup heavy cream**

½ **cup chocolate chips**

Everyone should have a go-to ganache recipe in his or her repertoire. This version is wonderfully effortless, and easy to remember. One part chocolate, one part cream. How simple is that?

1 Heat cream in a small saucepan over medium-low heat. Bring to just a simmer. Remove from heat.

2 Add the chocolate chips to the hot cream. Allow to sit for 30 seconds. Stir until well combined.

MILK OR DARK?

Feel free to use any type of chocolate you choose in this recipe, be it milk chocolate, dark chocolate, or even bittersweet. Avoid unsweetened chocolate, however, as you may find it too bitter without the addition of a sweetener.

Simple
Marshmallow
Syrup

Yields: 1 cup

INGREDIENTS

1½ cups Marshmallow Fluff

¼ teaspoon vanilla extract

2 tablespoons boiling water

This easy syrup is used in several recipes throughout this cookbook, from pancakes to bread pudding, and even as a topping for coffee cake. It's very versatile, so expect to use it often.

Combine the fluff, vanilla, and boiling water in a small bowl. Use as desired.

Homemade
Graham Crackers

Yields: 1 cup

INGREDIENTS

1½ cups whole-wheat flour

½ cup graham flour

1 cup all-purpose flour

½ teaspoon salt

½ teaspoon baking soda

1 teaspoon baking powder

1 stick unsalted butter

½ cup sugar

2 tablespoons molasses

¼ cup honey

2 teaspoons vanilla extract

½ cup buttermilk

The foundation of all things s'mores—it's hard to have a great one without graham crackers! While it's certainly easy to buy a box at the store, you'll find it well worth your time and effort to make your own. These are rich, buttery, and wonderfully delicious.

1 Whisk the flours, salt, baking soda, and baking powder together. Set aside.

2 Beat the butter, sugar, molasses, honey, and vanilla on medium-high speed until light and fluffy. Turn to low and add the flour mixture and buttermilk in alternating batches, starting and ending with the flour mixture. Cover and refrigerate 4 hours to overnight.

3 Preheat the oven to 350°F. Roll the dough out to about an ⅛"-thick rectangle. (You might need to divide the dough up to make it more manageable.) Cut into squares and place on cookie sheets.

4 Poke holes into the top of each square and bake for 15 minutes or until just slightly more golden brown. Cool on wire racks.

Homemade
Marshmallows

Yields: 64 (1") marshmallows

INGREDIENTS

¾ cup water, divided

2¼ teaspoons unflavored gelatin

⅔ cup light corn syrup

2 cups granulated sugar

1 tablespoon vanilla extract

¼ teaspoon almond extract

¼ cup powdered sugar

¼ cup cornstarch

Until you've had a homemade marshmallow, you've not *had* a marshmallow! These are soft, airy, and full of incredible flavor. As if that weren't enough, they are perfect for s'mores-making, as you can cut them into any shape or size you want.

1 Line an 8" × 8" square pan with foil. Lightly grease the foil and set aside.

2 Pour ½ cup water in a mixing bowl and sprinkle gelatin over the top. Turn the mixer on low and allow to bloom for 5–10 minutes.

3 While the gelatin blooms, boil the remaining ¼ cup water, corn syrup, and sugar over medium heat. Continue to boil for 1½ minutes.

4 Pour the hot sugar mixture slowly into the gelatin mixture while the mixer is on low. When everything is incorporated, turn up to medium high and whip for 5 minutes. Add the vanilla and almond extracts. Turn up to high and whip for another 7 minutes or until the mixture has tripled in volume and will form stiff peaks when the mixture is lifted out of the bowl.

5 Quickly spread into the prepared pan. Sprinkle the top with a dusting of powdered sugar and cornstarch. Allow to set for 3–4 hours.

6 Remove marshmallows from the pan and cut with a well-oiled knife or well-oiled pizza cutter.

Marshmallow
Frosting

 **Yields:** approximately 3 cups

INGREDIENTS

3 egg whites

1¾ cups granulated sugar

⅓ cup water

2 teaspoons light corn syrup

2 teaspoons vanilla extract

1½ cups mini marshmallows

Thick, sweet, and marvelously marshmallowy, this frosting is essential in creating the perfect s'mores ensemble. Cupcakes and layer cakes never had it so good!

1 Place about 3" of water in a very large pot and bring to a high simmer.

2 Place the egg whites, sugar, ⅓ cup water, and corn syrup in a metal or glass bowl fitted over the pot of simmering water.

3 Beat constantly with an electric mixer while over the boiling water until stiff peaks form, about 8–15 minutes. Remove from heat.

4 Fold in the vanilla and marshmallows. Beat with the mixer on high until the marshmallows melt. Use as desired.

Homemade
Chocolate Syrup

Yields: 2 cups

INGREDIENTS

½ cup cocoa powder

1 cup water

2 cups sugar

Pinch salt

½ teaspoon vanilla

It's always a good idea to have a jar of chocolate syrup on hand, as it can be used in a variety of ways. From a special treat over waffles to the perfect sundae topping, and especially as a garnish on many desserts, chocolate syrup is the ideal sweet kitchen staple.

1 Combine the cocoa powder and water in a saucepan over medium heat until the cocoa is dissolved. Slowly add the sugar, and continue to stir. Bring to a boil for about 3 minutes, then add the salt and the vanilla. Allow to cool.

2 Use immediately, or pour into a sterilized glass jar. Keep stored in the refrigerator. This recipe keeps for several months.

SYRUP TIPS

Homemade chocolate syrup, once cooled, should be stored in a sterilized glass jar in the refrigerator. Stored properly, it will keep for up to 6 months. In addition, if you have access to flavorings other than vanilla, feel free to use them in this recipe to change up the syrup with an unexpected flavor punch. Raspberry, strawberry, orange, banana, mint, or coconut extract would all be wonderful exchanges.

Chocolate
Pudding

Yields: approximately 6 cups

INGREDIENTS

¼ cup granulated sugar

¼ cup light brown sugar

2 tablespoons cornstarch

⅓ cup cocoa powder

2 cups whole milk

2 cups half-and-half

1 cup chocolate chips

¼ cup unsalted butter, cut into 1" chunks

1 tablespoon vanilla extract

Silky chocolate pudding is amazing on its own, but when used in the s'mores desserts found in this cookbook, you have a new degree of delicious. Try it in the Mini S'mores Trifles (see Chapter 5) or the S'mores Puff Pastry Mini Tarts (see Chapter 4). Both are incredible!

1 In a medium pot, stir the sugars, cornstarch, and cocoa powder until well combined.

2 Slowly whisk the milk and half-and-half into the mixture, then bring to a boil, whisking vigorously until thick.

3 Whisk in the chocolate chips and butter until fully incorporated and smooth. Whisk in the vanilla. Pour into a heatproof bowl. Cover the surface with plastic wrap and refrigerate 4–8 hours.

Index

Note: Page numbers in *italics* include photographs.

Standard U.S./Metric Measurement Conversions

VOLUME CONVERSIONS

U.S. Volume Measure	Metric Equivalent
⅛ teaspoon	0.5 milliliter
¼ teaspoon	1 milliliter
½ teaspoon	2 milliliters
1 teaspoon	5 milliliters
½ tablespoon	7 milliliters
1 tablespoon (3 teaspoons)	15 milliliters
2 tablespoons (1 fluid ounce)	30 milliliters
¼ cup (4 tablespoons)	60 milliliters
⅓ cup	90 milliliters
½ cup (4 fluid ounces)	125 milliliters
⅔ cup	160 milliliters
¾ cup (6 fluid ounces)	180 milliliters
1 cup (16 tablespoons)	250 milliliters
1 pint (2 cups)	500 milliliters
1 quart (4 cups)	1 liter (about)

WEIGHT CONVERSIONS

U.S. Weight Measure	Metric Equivalent
½ ounce	15 grams
1 ounce	30 grams
2 ounces	60 grams
3 ounces	85 grams
¼ pound (4 ounces)	115 grams
½ pound (8 ounces)	225 grams
¾ pound (12 ounces)	340 grams
1 pound (16 ounces)	454 grams

OVEN TEMPERATURE CONVERSIONS

Degrees Fahrenheit	Degrees Celsius
200 degrees F	95 degrees C
250 degrees F	120 degrees C
275 degrees F	135 degrees C
300 degrees F	150 degrees C
325 degrees F	160 degrees C
350 degrees F	180 degrees C
375 degrees F	190 degrees C
400 degrees F	205 degrees C
425 degrees F	220 degrees C
450 degrees F	230 degrees C

BAKING PAN SIZES

U.S.	Metric
8 x 1½ inch round baking pan	20 x 4 cm cake tin
9 x 1½ inch round baking pan	23 x 3.5 cm cake tin
11 x 7 x 1½ inch baking pan	28 x 18 x 4 cm baking tin
13 x 9 x 2 inch baking pan	30 x 20 x 5 cm baking tin
2 quart rectangular baking dish	30 x 20 x 3 cm baking tin
15 x 10 x 2 inch baking pan	30 x 25 x 2 cm baking tin (Swiss roll tin)
9 inch pie plate	22 x 4 or 23 x 4 cm pie plate
7 or 8 inch springform pan	18 or 20 cm springform or loose bottom cake tin
9 x 5 x 3 inch loaf pan	23 x 13 x 7 cm or 2 lb narrow loaf or pâté tin
1½ quart casserole	1.5 liter casserole
2 quart casserole	2 liter casserole

About the Author

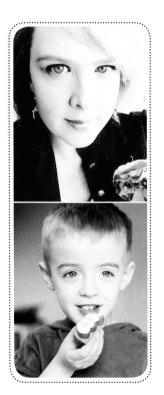

Susan Whetzel is a professional baker, food blogger, and award-winning recipe developer for major brands, including Hershey's, Dixie Crystals Sugar, KitchenAid, and more. Her blog, Doughmesstic.com, has been featured on several high-profile cooking websites, including BettyCrocker.com, MarthaStewart.com, *Bon Appétit*, *Taste of Home* magazine, and Walmart.com, among others. She also works as a brand ambassador for many food and cooking companies, and writes for a regional magazine. Susan is a wife and mother to a five-year-old little boy who, of course, loves s'mores. *The S'mores Cookbook* is Susan's third published cookbook, and by far her favorite. She lives in Pearisburg, Virginia.